How to Avoid Fucking Up at College

Matthew J. McCarthy

Published by Matthew J. McCarthy, 2022.

HOW TO AVOID FUCKING UP AT COLLEGE

First edition. April 11, 2022.

Copyright © 2022 Matthew J. McCarthy.

ISBN: 979-8835102204

Written by Matthew J. McCarthy.

Table of Contents

Title Page 1
Copyright Page 2
Dedication..7
How to Avoid Fucking Up at College 8
Forward...9
How I Failed Out of College, Twice 11
Are Today's College Students Entitled Little Shits?.............17
Should You Even Bother with College?................................18
Does Community College Suck?...21
Will You Get a Shitty Professor in College?.........................24
What if You Can't Decide on a Major?..................................27
Are College Rankings Worth Considering? 31
Who Gets to Choose the University? 33
Does Going to an Out-of-State 'State' University Make Sense? 34
Should Homesickness Be Considered in Your College Choice? 35
Are College Amenities Important?...36
Is it OK to Settle on Your 'Safety' School? 37
Should You Take Out a Student Loan? 38
Do Some Colleges Abuse Student Loans? 40
Should You Tour Your Campus First? 42
When Does College Failure Begin? 44
Can You Recover if you Fail a First-Year Class? 47
Should You Double Major?..49
Is College Accreditation Important?......................................51
Are You Too Immature for College? 53
Will You Send Cringy Emails to a Professor? 56
Do Mature Students Fail Too?...59
Is Time Management a Big Deal? 61
Is it OK to Miss Class in College? 63
Are There People Trying to take Advantage of You on Campus? ...65
Is the 'Freshman 15' Real?...67
Why Aren't You Sitting in the Front of the Class? 68
Is it Safe on a College Campus?..70
Should You Reboot When You Arrive on Campus?...............71
Do You Need to Make Friends the Day You Arrive on Campus? ...72

Should You Start a Study Group? 73
Nothing Good Happens After Midnight..75
Take Time for Yourself..78
Should You Join a College Club?..79
Should You Take Advantage of Summer School at Community
College? 81
Should You Take any Self-Paced or Online Classes? 83
Why Would You Take Online Classes? 85
What Happens if You Drop a Class?..87
Are Student-Athletes Good Students? 89
Do Excuses Work in College?...90
Should You Fear Finals Week? 92
What if You Just Plain Suck at Exams? 94
What are the Best Study Tips I've Ever Heard?...............................95
What Happens When You Cheat in College? 97
The Worst College Advice I Ever Gave 99
Conclusion 103
Important: What to Do if an Active Shooter Event Takes Place on
Campus 104

Nancy Ann, smooch

Forward

For most people, college is a significant investment with an important caveat: You need to graduate to reap the benefits. But college graduation rates are not favorable. Consider the following:

- More than one million students drop out of college every year, and three-quarters of them are first-generation college students. (Source: *Forbes*)
- At four-year colleges, 40% of undergraduate students drop out. (Source: Education Data Initiative)
- Black students have the highest dropout rate at 54%. (Source: Education Data Initiative)
- Nearly one-third of first-year college students drop out before their sophomore year. (Source: Education Data Initiative)
- Students who drop out of college are nearly 100 times more likely to default on their student loans than graduate students. (Source: Mark Kantrowitz at *Forbes*)
- The earnings lost from dropping out of college is $3.8 billion in a single year. (Source: Education Data Initiative)

Do I have your attention?

One person who takes these statistics seriously is Matt McCarthy, a multi-award-winning professor at Arizona State University. Having taught more than 70,000 students in his career, McCarthy has seen what separates people who complete college from those who drop out. What helps is that McCarthy nearly became a dropout statistic, so he has seen what causes students to drop out from multiple vantage points: as a student, professor, and parent.

McCarthy uses numerous — and often hilarious — examples to drive home the lessons about what differentiates a college graduate from a college dropout. With his engaging writing style, McCarthy shares fundamental truths in a way that's accessible to students and their parents. By adopting the lessons in these pages, a student is more likely to graduate and realize the rewards.

This book is the most valuable gift that family and loved ones can give to current or prospective college students.

Gregory S. Dawson, Ph.D.

How I Failed Out of College, Twice

Why would you take college advice from me? I failed university twice, once in spectacular fashion. Now imagine me teaching full-time at one of the most prestigious business schools in the world to the largest face-to-face classes at the largest public university in the country.

My life at university revolves around cavernous lecture halls named after forgotten benefactors that hold up to 400 first-year college students at a time. I teach these large classes nine times a week, all with my hair on fire, or at least what's left of it. You read that right: 3,600 first-year students every fall. That's somewhere north of 70,000 students I've taught since I started my academic career. Yeah, I'm that guy. You either took my class or one like it or will undoubtedly take a core business class like mine when you begin your college career.

Every day before my lecture, I check my fly, charge the battery in my microphone, and caffeinate to the gills. Every day, I also look for someone like me, the kids who, for one reason or another, are going to fuck up at university as severely as I did.

How did I flunk out of college, ending my university experience in a short 16 weeks after posting an extraordinary 1.2 GPA? How was I kicked so far out of university that they didn't even offer me academic probation? Even had I been given academic probation, my parents had had enough of my bullshit. That was the last time they would pay for my tuition. In a blur, my academic career was over. Less than a week later, my shitty report card showed up at my parent's house in late December. After that, I worked full-time at a full-service gas station, exiled to a ramshackle studio apartment with college disappearing in my rear-view mirror.

The first time I bombed out was a combination of pure apathy and beer, which sounds like a great band name. (Who wouldn't buy tickets to that show?) I wanted to be anywhere else but college. The problem was, I had no idea where that was. It wasn't as if I didn't think about my options after high school; I did. Like many 18-year-olds, I was convinced that I knew everything there was to know, and whatever I didn't know wasn't worth knowing. But underneath my unearned self-importance was an ever-present insidious feeling of dread that worsened as the 16-week semester counted down. I knew no descent professor would listen to my well-rehearsed, bullshit rationalization of why I missed several classes and assignments. So, what was the point?

Throwing myself at the mercy of the faculty court wasn't going to work either. It wasn't that I couldn't handle the classes. I just wasn't going to class. I knew the consequences of flunking out, but I would deal with them later. In the meantime, I would enjoy everything college had to offer, with one exception: academics. And when I failed, my parents were deeply disappointed, maybe something closer to devastated. I had failed so badly that my failure was their failure, and their failure cut them deep, and I knew it. Congratulations, you're the first and only person in your family to flunk out of college.

After a few years of busting my ass at the gas station, I got the notion that I would go back to university and finish what I'd started. I couldn't afford beer anymore; I no longer lived in the dorms with endless distractions and was now married. I began to embrace that I didn't know shit from Shinola, and my unearned ego was dissipating fast. More importantly, I finally knew what I wanted to be, or I thought so. Asking my parents for tuition money was never an option. I knew they would give me the money, but my pride wouldn't allow it. I never told them I was going back to the university; I didn't tell anyone.

Keep in mind that this all happened during the University Cretaceous Period when many professors were roaming campus wearing elbow-patched tweed jackets with dog-eared briefcases. Smoking cigarettes indoors passed as mundane (even during class). Back then, night classes were few and far between and typically never the ones I needed. The internet was a decade away. Back then, it also meant a specific course required for my major might have only been offered once a week and often in the middle of the day. Not exactly conducive for a full-time grease monkey living off hourly wages. I couldn't ask my boss if I could leave work for a couple of hours in the middle of a shift to drive down to Big State U and take my macroeconomics class.

I hung tough for six or seven semesters until reality intervened. I could either quit working altogether (which I couldn't afford) and give the school the full attention it deserved or fail again. I chose failure. I gave up. Honestly, I was relieved. A weight had been lifted from me. Failure felt right.

So how does a two-time flunky end up teaching in a prestigious business school? During my second or third mid-life crisis, the university bug bit again; don't ask me why because I have no idea. At this point in my life, a degree didn't matter anyway. I was a successful enterprise database consultant finding more contract work with Fortune 500 companies than I could take. My main contract was with a global behemoth that was said to be "too big to fail." (We all know how that story ended.) Once I had built their database, all I had to do was wait for it to break. The behemoth paid me to sit around and wait alone at home. Let me tell you, cabin fever is real. Your friends are at work, there's no one to play with, you're golfing alone, and you're bored enough to chat with the extended car warranty guy who cold-called. The poor guy is trying desperately to get you off the phone. It's soul-crushing.

Without noticing, the Cretaceous had given way to the Neolithic. Like banks who'd seen a future in ATMs, universities started to understand that their students were customers. Classes were now offered at all hours of the day and night. Universities also started embracing the preposterous notion of online classes. I only needed 18 lower-division elective credits to complete my undergraduate degree. I needed something to do because the stupid database system I'd built for my corporate overlords refused to break.

Moreover, I needed to do something fulfilling and rewarding. I signed up for 18 credit hours consisting of six concurrent eight-week online classes from an accredited university. I thought I was years away from a diploma. But I tapped my ruby slippers together and worked my ass off. Six weeks later, my business diploma appeared magically on my front porch in a tidy FedEx envelope.

I had finally accomplished something. Now I wanted more. I became insatiable. I didn't want only a master's degree, I wanted a Ph.D., so maybe I could become a college professor. Perhaps I could pull it off so my parents could live to see it. My parents are

13

incredibly proud of all their children, including me. Two weeks after receiving my undergraduate degree, I had some tough decisions.

Even though universities had slithered out of the primordial soup by embracing online classes, they were anything but perfect. The online courses for my master's degree were tied to traditional semesters. That meant the online courses I needed had to be available in a particular semester. If not, I would have to wait until the next semester started for them to become available. Some classes were only given once a year. I could either get my master's degree in three years by chipping away in online courses here and there or dive in headfirst.

Luckily, the stars aligned, and every class I needed was given within a calendar year. But that meant becoming a full-time student with a full-time class schedule. I started to worry about the stupid database breaking because I wouldn't have the time to fix it. I rolled the dice and decided. After 354 days of intensive fall, winter, and spring semester classes, another FedEx envelope was sitting on my porch.

With a master's degree in hand, I brazenly drove down to the local state university unannounced to sign up for a Ph.D. program. I didn't write. I didn't call. I just showed up uninvited to convey my seriousness. I wanted to tell them about my successful consultancy where I'd pick and choose Fortune 500 companies wanting to hire me because my databases never broke. I wanted to show them obscure database journals where my work was published. I wanted data dorks to read my new and exciting database techniques on how to make unbreakable databases. I tried to tell them about my master's degree, where I had graduated with distinction at the top of my class in only 354 days.

Within 10 minutes, they inferred I wasn't whom they were looking for in a Ph.D. candidate. They wouldn't even let me fill out an application. I drove home disheartened, gripping my steering wheel hard from anger and humiliation. My hands became numb. I was screaming to myself, winning imaginary arguments with them. Who did they think they were, and why were they making a huge mistake? Who were they to deny me a chance? I thought universities were supposed to think outside the box. Was that just a bullshit slogan they printed on some shiny college brochure? How will I be able to teach at university if I can't get a Ph.D.?

I called the business school dean to rake him over the coals when I got home. I found his phone number on their Neolithic website and formulated two things I wanted to tell him in order of importance: First, this is bullshit! I should be judged on my merits and apply as a Ph.D. candidate. (After all, my databases never break!) Second, I want to teach at your university someday. I dialed the number and was immediately caught off guard because he'd answered the phone. Who does that? I was further caught off guard because he was disarming, attentive, and astute. After a few minutes, he asked if it was OK to transfer me to the head of the department where I hoped I would eventually teach. (The same department that denied me from applying to get into their Ph.D. program about an hour earlier.)

After the dean transferred me to someone new, a friendly voice answered the phone, and I considered giving him a piece of my mind; after all, I had rehearsed it in my car all the way home. After hearing my qualifications, I told him that I wanted to teach at his university someday. What he said next knocked me off my feet. He calmly said that I didn't need a Ph.D. to teach. What came next was even more mind-blowing. He asked if I knew the local deli on the east side of campus. I did. He asked if he could meet there the next day to interview me for a full-time teaching position. Wait, what? The next day something extraordinary happened while sitting in front of a half-eaten bacon, lettuce, and tomato sandwich. He offered me a full-time teaching job that has now spanned over two decades. I had gone from high school graduate to teaching in one of the more prestigious business schools in the world in just over a year.

All's well that ends well, right? If you think this is a story of perseverance and redemption, you'd be dead wrong. It's a cautionary nightmare about lethargy, endless frustration, unnecessary struggles, missed opportunities, thousands of dollars wasted, deep humiliation, and an insane amount of luck. I shouldn't be here. So, what is my point?

I usually think it's a terrible idea to speak from authority, but you'll have to indulge me. After making every conceivable mistake in college and teaching tens of thousands of first-semester freshmen face-to-face over two decades, I may be one of the most qualified people to give college advice for a successful and fulfilling university experience. I've seen it all.

15

This is not hyperbole, it's genuine, and I wish it were untrue. In my years at university, I've seen many gifted young people fail out of college, crying uncontrollably in my office at the end of a semester, about to lose their scholarships. They leave school while still on the hook for non-forgivable student loans that remind them of failure every month when their payment gets deducted from the bank. It was all avoidable. None of this had to happen if these students knew a few things they don't teach in high school or college. Maybe that's too real, like the title of this book.

What follows are not tips and tricks for a successful college career. There are no tricks. This is real-world, proven advice for getting the outcome you deserve from your university journey. This book is for high schoolers, their parents, and college students. It's also written in a particular order, from thinking about college to getting there, and then real-world advice to keep you there and get a successful outcome.

Are Today's College Students Entitled Little Shits?

Before you dive in, let me dispel one of the most common myths about today's college students. To give you context of where I'm coming from, the No. 1 question I get when people find out what I do for a living: Are today's college students entitled little shits? I can see why people think every college student is an entitled butthole.

While corporate news has been trying to survive, it's been crapping on the younger generation every chance it gets. A standard news formula roots out the deviance in society, representing it as the norm and scaring viewers almost every newscast. You know the drill. The newscast interviews a pretentious, entitled student from Eastern Prestigious Exclusive University on camera and infers that every student is the same. I'm used to the question by now. Still, I'm not sure most people are ready for my answer. In my experience, after seeing 70,000-plus students face-to-face, I can tell you without hesitation that most college students are exceptional. I've run into one or two little shits over the past couple of decades, but way less than you'd think. Today's college students are astonishing, and I'm often jealous of them. The future is bright.

Should You Even Bother with College?

Before heading to college, consider the following question: Why the hell do you want to go to college in the first place? It's an honest question. It's also a question that some high schoolers never consider. My parents insisted I go to college even when they could barely afford it, come hell or high water. I already had three siblings at university, so it seemed the logical next step. All my friends are going, so I'll follow the crowd. It was as if my first year at college was preordained the same way a third-grader articulates to the fourth. I was going from 12th grade to 13th — a big mistake.

I regret going to college immediately out of high school. I often wonder what it would have been like to have been a firefighter or joined the U. S. Coast Guard and jumped out of helicopters into the frigid Bering Sea to rescue wayward crab fishers. What about working for the National Park Service as a badass fire jumper or traveling the world with the Peace Corps and making a real difference? Maybe I could have been a plumber or carpenter. Unlike my college graduate peers, as a plumber, I would have started my career four years earlier as a journeyman. Maybe I'd have a couple of bucks in the bank. Perhaps I'd have no endless student loan repayments looming on the horizon and possibly even a paid-off Chevy Silverado or Ford F-250 truck sitting in my garage. What never occurred to me was that college wasn't going anywhere. It never occurred that many employers might have paid for college had I chosen to go later. It never occurred to me that college was just one path and that never going may have been a good idea.

Here's a list of culprits that kept me from considering not going to college, beginning with me. I suffer from severe FOMO (fear of missing out) — even today. I thought missing out on college and not being with my friend groups might have been fatal. There was nothing I was addicted to more than people's approval. I can even trace some of my life's achievements directly to peer pressure. The funny thing about peer pressure is that none of my peers pressured me. Seeking approval and praise was *my* drug of choice. If my friends were heading to college, so was I, no questions asked. The gang would get back together in the first year of college, and we'd rule the campus like we did when we were seniors in high school. But college isn't anything like high school. Like so many drugs, FOMO had robbed me of what little critical thinking skills I had and the endless options to consider other than college.

Culture and perceived stigma also robbed me of my senses or to ignore so-called "trade" vocations like plumbing, heating, carpentry, etc. Have you ever heard a political candidate promise free college for anyone with a pulse? This promise adds to the stigma that you will never be successful if you don't go to college. It suggests that college is the end all be all. It's not. Are you saying I must pay for welding school or HVAC (heating, ventilating, and air conditioning) school out of my pocket while the elite attends college for free? Why not say free college and trade school? But I didn't want to be a plumber with his butt crack hanging out and his head under a kitchen sink. Besides, plumbing looks like hard work. Screw that! That's below me! Looking back, I'm ashamed I had those bigoted attitudes. How else did my close-minded, prejudiced attitudes blind me?

Perhaps the typical high school counselor is the person who ingrains that college is the only path. My high school counselor was no help. I found myself sitting in a circa World War II chair in his claustrophobic lead-painted office adorned with dingy college banners, and the first question he asked was, "What do you want to be when you grow up? Because if you know what you want to be, I have the college for you! Even if you don't see what you want to be, I have the college for you! I happen to have an application to Big State U right here on my desk!"

I've seen used car salespeople more subtle than my high school counselor. The great ones will open the world to you without pressure to attend college. You would think my high school counselor got a commission for every student he sent to the university. But just because I had a shitty high school counselor cruising to retirement doesn't mean you do.

Last thing: I'm not trying to talk you out of college. I'm not trying to talk you into college either. Let me say that going or not going to college is not a binary choice. Going to college is one of many options you can make coming out of high school. Open your mind, cast off preconceived notions, and make the best choice for yourself. I wish I had.

Does Community College Suck?

Often described as "two more years of high school" or low prestige, community colleges have suffered prejudicial and unfair characterizations throughout their history. No institution is more unfairly maligned and misunderstood than community college. In my experience, not going to the local community college was the single biggest mistake I made coming out of high school. I even turned down athletic scholarships to community colleges; it would have been free.

I get it. You wouldn't be caught dead on a community college campus because it's below you. You didn't bust your ass in high school to land at community college! You took AP classes for a reason. You can't wait to proudly wear your four-year university T-shirt after graduating from high school. That T-shirt with Big State U or Private University (that no one has heard of) emblazoned on your chest says a lot about you without saying a word. It tells everyone that you got into university. It says you punched the SAT in the neck and made it your bitch. It says you are a serious university scholar. It says you belong to a proud four-year tradition and enter the prestigious legacy of those who preceded you. It says you're all grown up. You deserve to wear your university's school colors. Besides, community college doesn't compare to the perceived four-year university experience.

Promise, I'm not trying to convince you to go to community college either. I'm not trying to convince you of anything. You do you. Instead, I will dispel some rumors and myths and point out some aspects of the community college that seem more secretive than the Da Vinci Code, beginning with cost. For perspective, community college tuition can be as little as $3,500 per year versus $35,000 for in-state students attending a public university. Of course, the numbers vary depending on your comparisons, but one thing is true: Community college is way less expensive than an in-state public university.

If community college is cheaper, it stands to reason that the education is inferior, right? That statement is patently stupid; nothing could be further from the truth. On the contrary, classes are often smaller and more flexible than public universities, and community college professors are more accessible and helpful. How do I know this, you ask? Because state law requires me to meet with my community college colleagues every year, sometimes twice a year, to compare notes, specifically to trade syllabi. Ask me why. Since you asked, I'll tell you; it's called equivalency.

Let me see if I can explain the enormous significance of equivalency through my experience. I didn't go to community college or accept their athletic scholarship because I thought I would attend for two years, get an associate degree, and then jump headfirst into whatever I would do for the rest of my life. That was it; school was over — no more teachers and books. Even if I decided to go to a four-year public university after community college, there was no way they would accept my community college credits. My ignorance, prejudicial views, and expectations of community college were so thoughtless that it was criminal. If I had only known about equivalency, coulda, shoulda, woulda. Here's what I desperately wished I'd known: The reason I meet with my community college colleagues is to guarantee the class I teach at Big State U is "equivalent" to the similar class they are teaching at the community college, thereby ensuring (by law) that the community college course credits will transfer to my university, guaranteed, no questions asked.

Here's the good part. Imagine that after two years of community college, you want to transfer to your state's four-year university and get junior status for a business degree. So what? How the hell are you supposed to know which classes you should take at community college even if their course credits are guaranteed to transfer? That's where the partnership between community colleges and four-year state universities enters.

There may be a community college program known as ABUS for aspiring business majors in many states. The "A" means associate degree, and "BUS" means business. Clever, huh? Your community college counselor will give you a major map on your first day, which outlines the 20 courses (60 credit hours) of business classes you will take for the next two years. (Don't worry, you get to pick some electives.) Once you've completed your two-year ABUS and received your associate degree, you get guaranteed automatic admittance into the four-year state university's business school with junior status as a business major. All 60 hours from your community college count toward your business degree — guaranteed! You've completed half of college.

How badly do you want that four-year university T-shirt? You got one hell of an education in only four years, with an associate degree and a four-year state university diploma. After two years of community college, you paid much less tuition, stayed local, and could work if you had to or wanted to. Mommy could still cook your meals and do your laundry, and you never paid for a dorm or shitty meal plan. You never endured a random, douche roommate.

Note: At the risk of going too far, I might as well go all the way. Here are some things you may not know. College professors say something like this: 10% of your students will take up 90% of your time. I tell you this because, in my experience, certain groups of students take up almost none of your time and are practically maintenance-free because they have their shit together. Specifically, they serve in the military; they're student-athletes and adult learners — they're community college transfers. That's not to say that 10% are knuckleheads. They're not, but there's something about the community college transfer student I can't put my finger on that makes them a pleasure to teach. Maybe it's two extra years of maturity. Who knows?

I know that the community college path is excellent, and maybe it's right for you. One thing is for sure; at the very least, community college deserves your careful consideration. Last note: Grade point average (GPA) doesn't transfer from community college to the four-year state university. You start with a clean slate GPA when entering the state university with junior status. Once you graduate from the four-year state university, your reported GPA on your transcript will only reflect the classes you took there, not from the community college. But I'm not telling you that your community college GPA doesn't matter, so you can cruise until you get to the four-year university.

Will You Get a Shitty Professor in College?

Have you ever had a shitty high school teacher? Me, too. Think you'll have a shitty college professor? Maybe, probably. I can still remember a particular professor I didn't appreciate when I went to college. No one liked him. Everyone was pretty sure he didn't like himself, and it showed. It was forever ago, and I can still tell you his first and last name, but I won't because I'm not that petty. This guy seemed burned out. Maybe his fourth wife left him. He always seemed so put out that he had to spend an hour and a half a week in class with us low-brow students that could never possibly appreciate the depth of his intellectual gifts. He seemed like such a butthole that no one was willing to ask questions in class; maybe that was his plan because it worked to perfection. He was a philosophy professor that proclaimed on the very first day of class that a third of the course would drop, a third would fail, and the other third would barely pass. He went on to say that it was almost impossible to get an A in his class. I'd always wondered why no one could get an A in his class. Did it ever occur to him that maybe he was a shitty professor? He wasn't providing a nurturing learning environment.

But there was one criticism you couldn't say about professor butthole; he wasn't unfair. He did what he said in his syllabus. Homework due dates were available at the beginning of the semester, his class rules and expectations were unambiguous, and his grading criteria were crystal clear. That's all well and good, but those are simply expectations of any professor. Sorry, not sorry that Tiffany left you for Luther from the antiquities department, but there is no excuse to foster a lousy learning environment because you're having a bad decade.

Hopefully, you'll never run into a poor professor at university, it's not all that common, and there are plenty of ways to avoid them.

But before you start the "avoidance" plan of a shitty professor, it's essential to understand what constitutes one.

Just because a professor is a harsh grader, seems unbending in their rules, and maybe has terrible breath, that doesn't make them bad. Some professors are legitimately strict because they desperately want you to get the greatest possible outcome from their class. On the other hand, you may get a professor with a sparkling personality, who's fun to be around, has minty fresh breath, and gives thought-provoking lectures. The problem is that Professor Sparkling rarely grades assignments on time, her exams don't include anything from the lecture, and her assignment directions seem like the instructions for a corner dresser from Ikea.

You can ask other students what they thought of a professor, but don't mistake "tough" for "shitty." Some of the most challenging professors I've ever had were the very best, and they never patronized but constantly challenged you to do better. I learned the most from my demanding professor's classes, and strangely enough, those were the classes where I got my highest grades. RateMyProfessors.com (RMP) is usually helpful to get a general idea of what other students thought about a particular professor. I don't know this for certain, but I'm 99% sure your university looks at RMP.

If you're still dissatisfied with a professor, maybe you think something is unfair, or the professor didn't grade something right. Before approaching the professor with a grievance, make sure you have all your ducks in a row. If you believe one of your assignments was graded incorrectly, there's a decent chance it was a simple mistake. No harm, no foul. If it's not a mistake and you still have a grievance, be prepared to point out the professor's grading criteria in their syllabus and make a lucid argument of why you think your assignment deserves another look. Neither you nor the professor should ever make it contentious when meeting. So, what happens if you talked with the professor rationally and she disagrees with you despite the evidence you presented?

Here's what you do before you decide to email the university president and threaten to expose your university's unfair grading policies to *The Wall Street Journal*: Complain at the departmental level. Most departments have a generalist who will arbitrate between you and the allegedly offending professor. A good generalist will consider all the facts and then make a fair decision. You could fill out an end-of-the-semester evaluation and say her grading criteria are unfair and even mention her bad breath, but what the hell good is that to you, the semester is over, and your grade is final.

What if You Can't Decide on a Major?

Should you go to college if you can't decide on a major? What are you going to be when you grow up? That question first comes from your 7-year-old self proudly announcing to Grandma that you want to be a veterinarian. Then the question comes during one of the most stressful conversations when you're a high schooler. As your high school career dwindles to an end, some would rather suffer through another awkward sex-ed talk with their mom than the dreaded "what do you want to be when you grow up?" talk; it can be that cringy and stressful when you genuinely don't know what to pick as a major.

Some people know what they want to be, like my older brother. He unwaveringly knew that he wanted to be a pilot from when he was a fetus and never deviated once. It's written in his DNA. Not only that, but he also understood the path to becoming a pilot ran squarely through a university, and it would take some arduous work. Guess what happened? He became a pilot.

On the other hand, one of my younger brothers thoughtfully decided that college was not for him and never went. He wanted to be a professional skier and general contractor, and guess what happened? He became a professional skier and general contractor.

One thing is inevitable if you choose to go to college; knowing what you want to study and declaring a major is one of the most significant advantages for a first-semester, first-year student, maybe the biggest. But what if you still don't know what major to declare? The time for attending university is drawing near, your stress is building, and you still don't know. Fast forward a few months into June. You're standing in some dank high school auditorium built during the Great Depression at your graduation commencement. You're wearing your goofy cap and itchy nylon dress, posing for pictures with grandma, who still thinks you want to be an astronaut or a veterinarian. She can't remember, and you still don't know. Some of your friends know, which makes it worse. Why does it seem like they have their shit together, and you don't?

Have you ever considered why you don't know? It's not that you don't have your shit together or that grandma will be disappointed. She'll still give you three dollars and a syrupy Hallmark card for graduation. You don't know because you're thinking. You don't know because you don't want to settle. You don't know because it feels like lying if you relent and pick a major. You don't know because if you choose some random major, you'll do poorly because your heart won't be in it. You probably don't understand what majors there are, and you're also likely unaware of the options. Relax, it's OK not to know what you're studying in college. You don't need a major to start at university, at least not right away. At some point, though, you will be required to declare a major.

Consider the numbers when pondering your major. You need 120 hours of specific classes to graduate in most majors at your typical garden-variety university. That means you will take five three-hour courses per semester (15 hours) for eight semesters, resulting in 120 hours. If you start your academic career with a known major, you will know what classes to take when you first start. Many universities call this a "major map." (Some universities use trimesters, but the result is generally the same.) One of the most significant advantages of knowing your major before starting is that every class you take will count toward your degree.

Most universities will gladly admit you as an "Undeclared" or "Exploratory" major if you haven't chosen one. That way, you can take all sorts of classes your first year of college to see what you like before committing to any major. It's a great idea in many ways, but it can have some unintended consequences.

For instance, what if you remain an undeclared or exploratory major for three semesters, complete 45 hours of classes, and finally decide you've found your passion. You've seen and heard enough to know you want to be an actuarial accountancy major. You make an appointment with one of the business school's advisors to sign up to find that only 15 of the 45 hours of classes you've already taken will count toward an actuarial accountancy degree. Who knew that the Zeitgeist Science Fiction Television Series class you took while undeclared wouldn't count toward that elusive actuarial accounting degree? You also find out that you're missing a lot of prerequisite and core business classes you need for your new major's required courses. Your dreams of working in the thrilling insurance industry are fading.

Am I saying undeclared and exploratory are bad? No. OK, maybe. I am saying that just because a university will admit you without a major doesn't mean you won't eventually have to declare one. If you want to know what a major is like, there are some excellent resources. The obvious one is a college advisor. Unfortunately, many of them can only tell you about the majors in the school where they work. Go to a business school advisor, and they can't tell you about the agriculture, English, or gender studies majors.

Contrary to popular belief, asking a college student, "What's your major?" isn't just a pickup line. Other students with declared majors are your best resource when deciding what major to declare. Maybe they hate their major and admit they made a huge mistake. Perhaps they love it. Perhaps they will regale you with lusty stories and the endless benefits of majoring in Canadian Film Theory.

Is it true that many students change their major in college? Somewhat. It's not unusual for college students to change their major one or two times, but there's a catch: They usually change majors within the same college. For example, it's not uncommon for a finance major to switch to an economics major within the business school. For the most part, both finance and economics generally have the same core classes early on, so changing majors isn't that big of a deal. But what if you decide to change your photography major to a business major after three or four semesters? Showing up to the business school with 60 hours of class credits from the school of fine arts will not go well. Although those 60 fine arts credit hours are valuable, they won't count much to the business school and vice versa. It will seem like you're starting college from scratch.

Ask anyone and everyone about their major, especially college students with declared majors. Ask the college advisor what kind of job a specific major will get you. Ask people who have graduated from college and have jobs connected to their major. Be rude; ask them how much money they make. Ask about expected salary if money is a deciding factor for choosing a major; colleges and universities track that sort of thing now.

I can't even count the number of times I've gotten in enormous trouble by asking other people's kids what they will major in when they get to college. To me, it's that important to get the conversation going early. A typical parental response is, "She's in the fricking seventh grade. Leave her alone!" That doesn't put me off my holy academic crusade. It's imperative to start thinking about what you want to study in college, even if you change your mind 10 times. OK, you don't have to start thinking about a major in the seventh grade, but I'm serious; somewhere around the middle of your sophomore year in high school would be ideal.

Are College Rankings Worth Considering?

Are rankings a top consideration when choosing a college? As an academic professional and parent, I can answer two ways. *U.S. News & World Report* and *The Princeton Review*, who determine rankings, will tell you that their incredibly flawed and radically skewed rankings are the most crucial consideration when choosing a college or university. That's a bunch of horse shit. As an academic professional, in my experience, rankings aren't even a top 10 consideration.

As a parent, college rankings might be a massive consideration if I get off by telling my friends at the next cocktail party that little Billy or Candice got into the top-ranked liberal arts program of universities located on the east coast above the Mason-Dixon line. I'm saying that I have enough money to send them to a so-called elite university. I live off other people's approval for my dopamine habit. Sorry, that's probably a little too harsh and insensitive. My bad, sorry. I'm as guilty as anyone getting caught up in bragging about my kids but chasing rankings to brag about your kids isn't worth it.

Look, bragging rights aside, you must figure out who ultimately will be impressed with university rankings and when they count, like possibly getting into a graduate program or impressing a human resources director and deciding which resumes deserve consideration for a job interview. Many decision-makers value and sometimes overvalue rankings. Higher rankings equal better quality of education, right? That's not an argument I'm willing to address, but I will say remarkable alumni come out of the highest and the lowest-ranked universities all over the country. It would be disingenuous for me to say college rankings don't count because they do, but understand you are always banking on someone else's opinion of a college or university. In my opinion, college and university rankings shouldn't be the end-all, be-all they are touted to be.

Who Gets to Choose the University?

I don't want to get off on a rant, but I am still pissed off at one of my kid's high school counselors, and that was years ago. I should let it go. One day, my youngest came home and announced she had narrowed her college choices down to two costly private universities on the east coast. Who gets to choose the university: the parents or the student? She was sure either university would be happy to offer her a full-ride academic scholarship. After all, she was valedictorian at her high school, and her high school counselor was rooting her on like a rabid cheerleader. Rah!

When her mother and I sat down with the high school counselor, we had some very pointed questions. How much does it cost to fly my kid to the east coast several times a year? You understand we have other kids, right? Why are you pushing expensive schools that cost more than buying a five-bedroom house in Boca Raton? Lastly, why are you playing our daughter at small forward instead of point guard on the basketball team? (Yep, she was the basketball coach, too.)

We should have been pissed off at ourselves. Our daughter's high school counselor was a rockstar at her job, and we were asleep at the wheel. The real problem was that we were sending mixed messages to our kids. On the one hand, we said choosing a college was completely her choice when it wasn't. Of course, we wanted her to go to the college she chose, but we desperately hoped she went where we wanted her to go for several reasons, specifically cost. It was entirely unfair to our daughter. What made it worse was that we didn't know what universities and colleges cost. Had we been more upfront, better educated, and more in touch with our kids, we could have avoided a lot of tears (ours).

Does Going to an Out-of-State 'State' University Make Sense?

Y ou want to go to the sunshine and attend an out-of-state "state" university, huh? You want to pay three times as much as your in-state state university charges for tuition, huh? OK, wait, I can barely make an argument of why you should pay out-of-state tuition to an out-of-state "state" university. Out-of-state tuition is no joke, way more than the cost of your in-state state university. I'm not even including ancillary expenses like plane tickets, dorms, meal plans, etc. Hell, you may as well go to an overpriced private university if you're going to spend that much. You're trying to convince me that the out-of-state state business school is three times better than the in-state business school? Good luck! Your girlfriend or boyfriend is going out of state? So? Do you want to spread your wings and get away from home? Try again. Grandpa went there, so you want to go there, too. Nice try. Sorry, none of these reasons are compelling enough to spend three times as much for out-of-state tuition versus your state university's in-state tuition.

The only reason I can vaguely think of going to an out-of-state state university is that you secured a full-ride scholarship. Otherwise, the in-state university in your state doesn't offer the major you want — and that's if you're dead set on a major the in-state state university doesn't offer. For instance, most Midwest state universities in the corn belt are not legendary for their dolphin studies and marine biology programs. On the other hand, some state universities don't offer animal husbandry or meat science degrees. Go figure.

Should Homesickness Be Considered in Your College Choice?

Should homesickness be a significant consideration when choosing a college or university? God, yes! Before deciding which college to attend, you need to have a very open and honest conversation about potential homesickness. For clarity, there's nothing wrong with being homesick; it happens to almost every college student, whether they care to admit it or not. But homesickness can be crippling even to the most dedicated student. In a world of mobile devices, FaceTime calls, texts, and Zoom is not always enough to make a home seem closer. It's tough enough to be cast into a strange, new college environment, but in my experience, debilitating homesickness happens at university way more often than you think. I'm not a doctor, but I have seen homesickness cause severe depression, anxiety, and even shame in college students. I have even seen university students drop out of college mid-semester to go home.

How can you solve or avoid homesickness? My truthful response is that I don't have all the answers. I would say that universities have mental health counseling centers on campus covered by tuition and fees. There's no shame or stigma attached to homesickness, and mental health counseling visits are beneficial, discreet, and undisclosed for privacy.

Are College Amenities Important?

Whether you think so or not, college amenities like state-of-the-art recreation centers and artisan student dining halls are essential when choosing a university, and no one knows that more than the university. Students realize they must hang around campus for 16 weeks, so it better look like a high-end Pilates studio than Hogwarts. In the past 15 years or so, universities have poured untold millions of dollars into university amenities, even showing them off on the homepages of their websites. Some more creative universities have napping centers, ball pits, golf simulators, climbing walls, and even private spas. Some people (probably significantly older people) question if university funds should be spent instead on libraries named after a dead Nobel Laureate no one remembers. Still, no one goes to college because they have a library. Universities are keenly aware that students need somewhere cool to hang out with lots of amenities that serve as shared, familiar meeting places for everyone. Yesterday's musty gyms with a few mismatched barbells and mausoleum-type libraries won't do, and they certainly don't draw in students, aka customers. Don't forget to check out the dorms and look closely. Old dorms with decrepit plumbing, poor lighting, and a county lockup's warmth don't make for a great college experience. (See the previous chapter, *Should Homesickness Be Considered in Your College Choice?*)

Is it OK to Settle on Your 'Safety' School?

Let me climb as high as I can on my soapbox because all my kids were encouraged by their high school counselors to fill out an application for a "safety" school. They were applying for the safety school just in case they didn't get into the universities they wanted. Don't worry; you'll never have to suffer the embarrassment of attending a safety school. Fill out the common application should the worst happen, and you must attend school with the trolls who didn't get into Northeastern Privileged Private University.

I will readily admit that the whole concept of safety school chaps my ass. The school I teach in is sometimes considered a safety school, the so-called rented mule amongst a herd of elite thoroughbred universities. Even with my fervent disdain for college rankings, I will hypocritically point out that the so-called safety school where I teach is highly ranked and one of the finest in the world. We need to judge schools on their merits.

Here's another big problem with the safety school concept. What if you don't get into your first, second, third, or fourth choice schools because you got wait-listed or outright rejected. Maybe you can't afford your first, second, third, or fourth choice, and the so-called safety school is where you land? Oh, the humanity! Now you get to start your college career where you never wanted to go in the first place. Oh, the humiliation of it all! You're not off to a great start if you're disappointed where you land. OK, I'll stop, promise, but a few more essential points to consider. Big State U, where I teach, offers more than 1,000 majors. Where I teach provides some of the lowest tuition rates in the country. Big State U's amenities and weather are some of the best in the country. OK, that's three things. I could go on, but I think you get my point.

Should You Take Out a Student Loan?

I promise I'm not patronizing, but to explain student loans, I need to start with the nature of how most loans work instead of a student loan. Think about buying a house with a mortgage loan from the bank. Mortgage loans are collateralized. If you go belly up on the loan and stop paying, the bank takes back your house (collateral) or forecloses. The bank doesn't want your home. The last thing the bank wants is to foreclose on your house. It's a shitshow and very costly for the bank. Once the bank forecloses, it must hire someone to fix the house, pay the property taxes, pay insurance to protect the home, and hire a realtor to sell the house (probably at a loss). The bank will probably lose money from the unrealized interest it was expecting to make from the original mortgage loan. That's why the credit check process for the prospective home buyer applying for the mortgage loan feels more like a colonoscopy. The mortgage lender wants to (almost) guarantee the borrower pays them back with interest.

Now think about the homeowner who had his home foreclosed. The most obvious point is that they no longer have the house, but there's more bad news: They also walked away from a boatload of money. They lose their original down payment (maybe their life's savings) and possible equity built up in the home. More bad news: The bank will report the foreclosure to the credit bureaus, which means the former homeowner can't get credit for the next several (typically seven) years. The point is that mortgage lenders protect themselves from the threat of foreclosure because their loans are collateralized. But here's the thing, someday, all this will be a bad memory. Eventually, the black marks from the foreclosure nightmare on your credit report will go away.

Now think about a student loan. Student loans are not collateralized. If you can't pay the student loan after completing college, there's nothing for the lender to take back, such as a house, car, or motorcycle. They can't put you in debtor's jail or make you pick up trash on the side of the freeway because that's not a thing anymore. Then why would any lending institution in their right mind lend a 17- or 18-year-old with zero credit history tens of thousands of dollars to go to university? How do student lending institutions protect themselves without collateral? Easy, they get the government to get the rules changed. Student loan lenders successfully argued that they should be allowed to have harsher laws with uncollateralized lenders. Without too much detail, student loan lenders have a clause that lets them pursue you forever.

The Interwebz is littered with countless ways to lower, defer, or even evade your student loan payments. Still, as the sun rises every morning, one way or another, you can never escape the black hole of seemingly endless student loan payments. Even discharging a student loan payment through bankruptcy is an act of God. Let me be clear; I am not discouraging student loans; I'm simply pointing out reality. In some instances, student loans can be a great idea but beware. Understand what you are borrowing.

Do Some Colleges Abuse Student Loans?

T he answer, unfortunately, is yes. Here's a true cautionary tale I heard from someone I knew working as a college entrance counselor at a mid-sized college. I'll just fast-forward to the end of the story: She quit her job (which was her very first job out of college) in nine months. She couldn't sleep, she couldn't live with herself, and she was losing her hair; in short, her conscience had gotten to her. When the college entrance counselor was trying to sleep at night, she would imagine students she'd advised finishing their degree but not finding a job with the exaggerated income her university promised. Further, she knew that the same student wouldn't be able to afford student loan repayments.

Everyone was very proud when she got her college entrance counselor job. Since she loves helping people, the job seemed like a natural fit. She would advise prospective students and help them navigate the university application process. Then she found out the dark truth: The university she was working for started encouraging her to overinflate, essentially lie about the value of their degrees. It gets worse: Many times, the first document she would hand a prospective student was a student loan application assuring them they would qualify.

Imagine that meeting from the perspective of the potential college student after sitting down with a predatory college entrance counselor; an hour earlier, they had zero ideas of how they would afford college or even if they would be able to attend college in their lifetime. After the meeting, they have secured the low-interest student loan they need for tuition and books, and all they need to do in college is work hard, and a high-paying job will be waiting at the end of the magical journey. Imagine the euphoria of that student. One minute, they can't afford college, and the next thing they know, they're proudly sitting in their first college class, blithely unaware that their future paycheck doesn't exist. They are stuck with a student loan payment they may never hope to pay off in a lifetime.

Don't get me wrong; student loans can be an incredible thing; they help people afford college who may not ever have been able to attend a university. Student loans can be a great and affordable instrument to lift people. But saying student loans are fantastic is like saying beer is awesome. Beer is enjoyable, but too much can be dangerous. My intention isn't to keep you from utilizing student loans, pinky promise. Drinking beer is up to you as well. I'm just saying to understand what you are getting into with student loans. It is critical to do a cost analysis for your potential student loan. Understand your return on investment. If you know how to use a spreadsheet, do it. If you don't, get help! Don't skip this step under any circumstances! Understand what your monthly student loan repayment will be to the penny. The hard part is going to be the variables. What will that potential job pay? How much are your future living expenses, and how will a student loan payment affect that? (By the way, she's doing great now. She reported the predatory college and is on to bigger and better things.)

Should You Tour Your Campus First?

On my first day of college, I got a traffic ticket from a university cop for changing lanes on my motorcycle in a traffic jam, so I started the day off late and way behind. I was lost on my first day of classes because I had never visited the campus. The campus was over a full square mile of similar-looking, poorly marked red-brick buildings. Thank God for my trusty map, as soaked from the rain as was I. Which way was north? When I finally found my way to class, I was very late. Not the best impression for my professors. Little did I know, my professors didn't care if I was late and were not going to repeat what I had missed. I couldn't hang around after class to ask about specifics, like where to get the textbook, because I would be late getting to my English 101 class across campus in the architecture building. Wait, what? Even had I chatted with the professor after class about details, she would have uttered the three most famous, repeated, and dreaded words in the history of universities: Read the syllabus! My first college failure had commenced.

So, should you tour the campus first? Am I being too subtle or just being sarcastic? Yes, and yes! You should visit multiple times if you can. There is no better way to learn about a university than following an overenthusiastic student tour guide making less than minimum wage walking backward the whole time simultaneously reciting critical dates about the university's founders. At the university I work at, you would think it's the line to get into the Jungle Cruise at Disneyland because it is so popular.

The typical campus tour consists of dads wearing dirty, white New Balance sneakers they got on sale at Costco, casing the place like diamond thieves. There are emotional moms on the verge of tears about to become empty nesters and their mortified, disinterested-looking sons or daughters trailing in the back of the pack paying more attention to smartphones. If you can't take the tour, go with your friends, go alone, do it. Make a day of it; make it an adventure. Find your classes ahead of time. Find out new and interesting facts like: Did you know Big State U has six Starbucks on campus? Campus tours are entirely worth it. You will see people from all walks of life, from all over the world. Last thing: Ask a ton of questions. Don't be shy.

When Does College Failure Begin?

Collegeᴸ failure begins on the first day. I have a few buddies who are rockstars in the professor business who teach upper-level students, and they tell me that they're tired of all the first-day introduction tap-dancing bullshit. So, they start lecturing on the first day of class. Yep, get your books out, kids. Here's chapter one! The syllabus is on the class dashboard; it's up to you to read it. Want to know what book we're using? You should have figured that out a week ago when I posted the syllabus before school started. The professors can get away with this because they're teaching upper-level students. They also do it to hit the ground running and don't feel like wasting a day repeating stuff upper-level students should already know. Do upper-level students bitch about this? When they're juniors and seniors, they know the drill and prepare for a first-day lecture.

When first-year first-semester students land on campus, my professor buddies and I will tell you that they're incredibly different from their seasoned second-, third-, and fourth-year predecessors. There're things they have never seen or experienced, like the first time they must sit next to a 47-year-old adult learner that smells of French onion soup in their Introduction to Peruvian literature class. That never happened to them in high school. They may have to walk three-quarters of a mile from one class to another in searing heat or freezing snowdrifts. Maybe they saw the school's marching band standing waist-deep in a fountain playing their tubas and beating their drums while being hazed on their way to class. Maybe they slept in a room the previous night with a stranger. Oh, wait, that's your new roommate, same thing. Everything is a brand-new experience for a first-semester first-year student.

The most significant difference between first-semester, first-year students, and upper-level students is that upper-level students almost instinctively understand the intangibles of the university. They already know where they're going, have a good idea about their professor's reputation, and even know many of their fellow students' reputations. Maybe the most significant thing they know is that college failure starts on the first day. Do you think I'm kidding?

I have the analytics. The colossal mistake is to miss the first day of class and not read the syllabus all the way through. No one likes reading the syllabus, and I, for one, hate writing them. Half the time, I feel like I need an attorney's help because, to a certain extent, a syllabus is a legal contract between the student, the class, and me. Without first-day attendance, first-semester first-year students will miss expectations, explanations, how the class dashboard works, what book to buy, policy clarifications, when the first assignment is due, etc. You get the picture. Imagine missing the first day as a first-semester first-year student and trying to figure all that out independently.

After missing the first day of class, trying to catch up is a Sisyphean nightmare. You remember Sisyphus, right? You were supposed to read about him in high school, remember? Sisyphus was a Greek god sentenced to roll boulders up a mountain for eternity, only to see them roll back down every time. Loosely speaking, a Sisyphean task is highly demanding and is an utterly fruitless challenge. It will feel like this if you miss the first day of class. Consider that most courses at university are generally linear. For example, university classes typically build on the previous week's lesson. You'd struggle with the concept of "how to spell words" if you missed the last class that taught the alphabet.

If you missed the first class of the semester, ask the professor to catch you up in their office *before* the next class. That's their job, bringing you a great outcome in their class. You should have absolutely no confusion heading into the second week of class. Find other people in your class, too. Ask them what you missed. **Note:** They're not going to be helpful if you thought it would be cool to blow off the first day because some kid told you nothing happens the first day.

Secret pro tip: Look at the professor's class schedule. You didn't hear this from me, but if you missed your professor's first-day Economics 101 session class held on Monday at 9 a.m., that same professor might be teaching the same session first-day Economics 101 class at 10:30 a.m. Attend the 10:30 session if you missed the 9 a.m. session, and if the professor takes the role, find them after class and play dumb and say that you thought you were supposed to be in the 9 a.m. session, and it will never happen again.

I think I beat this dead horse enough, but one more thing: Missing class the first day is where failure starts, or at the very least, an inferior grade in a class starts. Classes like Statistics 101 are linear because they lead into Statistics 102. Stats 102 would be a struggle if you did poorly in Stats 101. You get the picture. Now let's talk GPA (grade point average). Starting with a low GPA after your first two freshman semesters and trying to raise it for the next three years of university is like improving a low credit score; it is a long and arduous task and can feel Sisyphean. Here's something to consider: Your first year starts around August or September, and you finish up your first two semesters around May or June the following year. After those first two semesters, you did a phenomenal job if you have 30ish credit hours and a three-point something-plus GPA.

Can You Recover if you Fail a First-Year Class?

If you fail a required first-year core class in your declared major, start thinking about attending summer school or how to pay for the fifth year of college, as it can get that ugly. Introduction to Peruvian literature worked out because the French onion soup guy turned out to be an awesome person and was super helpful as a study group partner. I'm not talking about that; I'm talking about failing a core class required for your degree. For instance, everyone must take core classes like Introduction to Biology at a science school or Introduction to Business Concepts at a business school. These first-semester core classes are where you will most likely experience your first "giant lecture hall" course with what seems like millions of other students. Your school, by design, makes sure you take these "intro" core classes your first semester. If you don't, you will be at least a semester behind — and maybe even a year — according to your major map schedule of classes.

If you fail a core class in your major in your first semester, there is a glimmer of hope. You have two specific tasks: first, catching up with your classmate, and second, repairing your GPA. For instance, you know those friends that didn't fail the core class, you won't be seeing them in classes anymore because you failed and haven't fulfilled the requirements to take the next set of courses. If you want to avoid an extra semester or two in college, think summer school, possibly at the local community college that has an equivalent class. A community college is a great option, but there's one significant disadvantage, it won't help with your four-year university's GPA. Only equivalent community college class credits transfer to your four-year school, not your GPA. It doesn't matter if you get an A in the comparable community college class; it won't help repair your four-year university GPA.

So, do you want to catch up and repair your GPA simultaneously? Here's something to think about; retake the same class at your university, get an A, and your GPA will be on the mend. Here's the possibly good part: Let's say you got a failing grade in a core first-semester, first-year student class that resulted in a 0.0 GPA. That's going to seriously eff up your overall GPA. OK, so you retake the same course next semester and get an A, which represents a 4.0 GPA, good for you. Combine the failed first attempt with the successful second attempt, and your GPA averages out to a 2.0, still not excellent. However, many schools discard the failed first attempt in first-year core classes like it never happened. I'm not kidding, they don't take the first failed attempt's shitty GPA into account, and you've replaced the 0.0 with a 4.0. Your GPA won't reflect the failed class on your school transcript. Not all schools do this, but it's not uncommon; terms and conditions apply.

Let me be exceedingly clear, what I just laid out should never be considered a safety net. Catching up and repairing a GPA is double tough, possibly not an option, filled with lots of challenging work, potentially costly, and usually has a giant dose of humiliation mixed in.

Should You Double Major?

I love talking to students after class because it adds a personal touch to a class of 400. Students can get answers, like when the next assignment is due. For some unknown reason, many students ask my opinion on double majoring after class, being considerate not to hold up the entire class when the familiar sound of rustling backpacks and laptops close.

Have you ever had a class with "that guy" that has just one more question when the class is clearly over? Toward the end of every class, everyone has had enough of my song and dance and can't wait to get out the door, but I still ask if there are any more questions. Just when you think you've escaped, someone decides to ask a question that holds everyone up.

One semester, I had "that guy" in the form of a very diminutive young woman (call her Sarah) that never failed to ask the last question. She seemed oblivious to the audible groans of "Are you kidding? Are you serious?" or "C'mon!" coming from impatient students. The funny thing was, after holding up 399 other students every class, Sarah always spoke to me after every class anyway, or to be clear, spoke at me. I never minded that Sarah held everyone up; that's her prerogative. One day after class, Sarah told me she was a quadruple major. Since she was on a full-ride academic scholarship, Sarah figured she'd get her money's worth. I've never seen a quadruple major. Hell, I've never even heard of one. Here's the weird part, none of her four majors were related. It wasn't like she was doing accounting, finance, economics, and supply chain management, all under the umbrella of the business school that shared many core classes. Her four majors were completely unrelated. I figured it would take her seven or eight years to complete if she got there.

The legend of Sarah points out that you need to be extra thoughtful when deciding to become a double major. On the one hand, you're getting two degrees for one price, and hopefully in just

49

four years. On the other hand, that comfortable 15 hours a semester might balloon to 21ish, and those 120 hours you need for a diploma might inflate to 145. I'm not sure why so many students ask my opinion on double majoring because I'm not an advisor or a counselor. I ask the same questions to aspiring double majors. Why? Is there a particular job that requires both degrees? Do you understand the commitment it takes to double major? Have you talked to your parents or an advisor about it? When considering double majoring, ask yourself. You need a great reason to double major.

Many moons ago, I spoke to my niece because she was upset at university. She was a scholarship athlete and a double major in business and math. Because her majors were unrelated primarily, even though she was a great student, she was getting her ass handed to her in classes. As if that wasn't enough, she also had to contend with daily Lacrosse practice. She called me around midnight her time and told me she was super-stressed and felt ashamed that if she dropped one of the two majors, people would be disappointed. So, I asked her the one crucial question: Why are you double majoring? What kind of job requires a business/math combo? She didn't know. I asked her what was the point of double majoring then? She was relieved that she didn't know that either. She dropped math the next day, and her college experience got immeasurably better. She's now a nurse in an intensive care unit at a world-renowned hospital alongside my other niece. Go figure.

If you decide to double major, try to do it within the same college, like a business college with shared core classes. That's my opinion (take it or leave it). Understand what a double major will get you for the added time commitment. Is there a specific job you want that requires both? Will you be a more attractive candidate for a job than those who got a single major? Maybe. Will a double major make you smarter? Probably, maybe. Here's something else to consider: Many students wait until they're a sophomore to decide whether to become a double major instead of declaring it as a first-year student. That way, they're better informed on the value of a double major, what it provides to them specifically, what the commitment looks like, and have more university experience, allowing them to make a more rational decision.

Is College Accreditation Important?

Yes. Very. Imagine if you saw an advertisement for a university promoting a massive sale on tuition for all incoming freshmen? That seems tacky. Plus, what about your current student body, who might be pissed off because the tuition sale wasn't available when they started. Some unscrupulous universities — and there are some out there — have a solution. They rebrand their "huge tuition sale" and call it a scholarship. The new advertisement says, "You might qualify for thousands of dollars of scholarships!" Let me save you the suspense; you will undoubtedly qualify for their so-called scholarships thinly veiled as a tuition sale. The scholarship "sale" tactic is to get you in the door of the university while you unwittingly and proudly tell everyone who'll listen that you got an "academic" scholarship! That same dodgy school will probably upsell you on student loans as well. These are just a few telltale signs that a university is not on the up and up.

So how can you avoid these corrupt institutions other than noticing that their university's central administration office shares the same building with a payday loan service? Look for actual accreditation. For example, AACSB-accredited is the gold standard for business schools. From the AACSB website: AACSB accreditation (Association to Advance Collegiate Schools of Business) is known worldwide as the longest-standing, most recognized form of specialized accreditation that an institution and its business programs can earn. Accreditation is a voluntary, nongovernmental process that includes a rigorous external review of a school's mission, faculty qualifications, curricula, and ability to provide the highest-quality programs. All colleges and universities should have "gold standard" accreditation. Do your research; look for it.

Be careful, though; some smarmy universities self-accredit. I know of a chain of supposed quasi-medical schools that got together and started their accreditation organization to accredit themselves.

Isn't that convenient? It's not as unusual as you think. You need an official-sounding accreditation name with a good acronym, a bogus board of directors (one from each fake school), and an excellent graphic designer to make an official-looking seal.

Are You Too Immature for College?

If you're an immature person, think about staying home from university. Don't go. I mean it; you're probably not even close to being ready for university. I don't care about your perfect SAT score. Immature students sometimes fail badly. It worsens; immature students never seem to blame themselves for flunking out of college. They'll be sitting on a barstool 10 years later, regaling someone who doesn't give a shit about their perfect SAT score and something about their college professors being dicks. They'll brilliantly (in their mind at least) outline every reason why college is a bullshit scam and just a money grab. Maybe they'll head home later and wonder why their prank video YouTube channel has less than 100 subscribers after two years.

The immature student wrongly assumes college is just like high school. They've finally made it to university. Good for them. Seriously, it's a great accomplishment. You have my sincere congratulations but let me be as blunt as possible and just come right out and say, "**If you treat college like high school, you will certainly fail**." Even if you were a great student in high school, let me repeat, "If you treat college like high school, you will fail."

In one of his classics, John Steinbeck describes the same four men getting together every Saturday night for years to play poker, drink beer, and talk shit. Because they exclusively played only within their group, they all became only as adept as each other at poker and started to assume that they were all great poker players. They weren't. They were only great (so they thought) within their group, which doesn't necessarily translate to the outside world. The same trap happens to incoming first-year college students that were big fish in their high school pond. Being above average at your high school doesn't translate to being above average at university. When you arrive at university, treat yourself like a clean slate.

Ask yourself a few questions and do yourself a favor. Answer honestly. In high school, did you ever immaturely humiliate yourself by begging your high school teacher for a grade you didn't deserve because you screwed off the whole semester? Maybe you had mommy come in and beg for you? Did you ever ask your high school teacher if there was any extra credit you could complete to raise your grade on the last day of the semester? Are you overly concerned with your "drip" or "fit," or have you ever uttered the phrase, "No cap?" to an adult? Have you spoken to an adult and addressed them as "bruh" or "dude?" I ask because these are just a few telltale signs of immaturity in college. I've seen immature students more concerned with being "cool" when they show up on the first day of university, dressed like they're heading to an LA nightclub. They're wearing so much makeup that they'll need a belt sander to remove it later that night.

Do you want to see what a mature, successful college student looks like? Come into my colossal lecture hall during the final days of the semester when it's cold outside and look around. Successful students are easy to spot. Successful students look dead tired; they're rightfully cranky, and their hygiene has fallen off a cliff. No makeup or fancy hairstyles as far as the eye can see. In what my daughters tell me, women wear their hair up in a shitball, and guys wear gym shorts that I guarantee they slept in for the past three nights. They are not cool or uncool, and they couldn't give a shit what people think about their "drip." They understand that no one at university cares if they're cool, and it's a complete waste of time. They are rightfully protective and selfish in the pursuit of their degree. They are never embarrassed to ask questions or make comments in class. They sit up front and are always in the same seat all semester long. They show up and stay for the entire course, no matter how excruciatingly boring a lecture might be. They know the world is run by those that show up. They all get their degrees on time and always come away from university with more than just class knowledge.

Now look again at the lecture hall at the end of the semester. Why are there so many empty seats? That's where all the cool kids used to sit. Many know that they have already failed mathematically, so why go. Maybe they subscribe to the philosophy that "Cs get degrees." (That's a thing.) They thought it was cool to tell their friends they skipped class and then try to leach off those same students who went to class for answers to the last quiz. Immature students pepper me with the early semester, Sunday night emails asking if they missed anything important in class the day they skipped. Do you have any idea how hard it is not to send back a scalding, sarcastic email explaining that we didn't do much of anything important the day they skipped? But I never do. Plus, I hate wasting good sarcasm. Those same students harangue me with late semester emails and office visits, hoping I curve grades, asking if there is any extra credit, begging if there is anything they can do not to fail, the same way they begged their high school teachers.

Will You Send Cringy Emails to a Professor?

Lt's not hard to correlate immaturity and college failure, so just a few more things: Are immature people aware that they're immature? Let me give you an example of a "false maturity" scenario in the form of emails I get every semester. It's typically an overly self-assured, subtly veiled demand that goes something like this:

Dear professor,

My name is blah blah blah, and I'm in your 10:30 a.m. class. You have probably noticed me; I was the one wearing the matching Fendi sweatsuit yesterday. Anyhoos, I have been extremely busy with other courses and many commitments to my sorority, of which I am our recruitment coordinator, a job I take very seriously. I didn't attend class this week with everything going on (Greek Week is next week!), and I couldn't complete this week's assignment. I should finish your assignment next week, so I'll need you to extend the deadline. Thanks in advance.

Sincerely,

Blah blah blah

I'm going to let you reply to this email. Your first instinct might be to return a hell and brimstone sermon about time management and that you don't give a rat's ass about whatever "Greek Week" is. You might continue your scorched earth tirade asking why every other class but yours is more of a priority. It's insulting! You might interlace your email with biting sarcasm and disdain. You might ask why in God's name do you think I care about your Fendi drip? As for your demand for me to grant you an extension, there's no effing way! Here's the reality of how I respond to this type of email:

Dear blah blah blah,

I post assignment deadlines at the beginning of the semester, so I will not be extending the deadline.

It's that easy. Who am I to question students' priorities even if they prioritize their sorority, Greek week, other classes, or Fendi over my course? The hell and brimstone sermon doesn't serve anyone. You're in college now, capable of your decisions.

Another false maturity email I get is the "Mia Culpa" approach that goes something like this:

Dear professor,

How are you doing? I hope you had a wonderful weekend. I have loved your class this semester, and it's been my favorite, TBH [to be honest]. My failing grade in your class this semester does not reflect who I am as a person and please understand that I am a very dedicated student. Academics are important to me, as are my grades. I know that my grade is my responsibility. I shouldn't have missed so many classes and assignments. It is entirely my fault, and I should have been more dedicated. I know it's the last day of the semester, so please let me know what we can do to rectify this situation.

Sincerely,

Blah blah blah

Your turn again. You get to handle this email, too. You may write something like, "Dear blah blah blah, if you were a truly dedicated student, you would have passed my class with flying colors, and we wouldn't be having this conversation. There is no 'situation' to rectify. Stop fooling yourself; you are not a dedicated student. Plus, you are so damn tired at the end of the semester that you can't summon the energy or words.

Here's the reality of how I respond to this type of email:

Dear blah blah blah,

I'm sorry your semester went poorly. The grades I have posted are final. You can retake my class next semester. I'm looking forward to seeing you there. Have a great winter break.

Sincerely

Me

You may wrongly assume my email responses are indifferent, unfeeling, or even obtuse, but I treat my university students like adults; this is college, not high school. I have made plenty of mistakes as an academic professional. I thought it was good to bring my dog to class because he was thoroughly potty trained; it was a literal shitshow. Never again. But one of the biggest mistakes I made early in my career, my first semester, was having what I like to call

Professor Santa Claus Syndrome. I grant the crying student their wish, their troubles are over, and there won't be any awkward conversation about failing with their parents over winter break. You can see the weight come off the student's shoulders and everyone, including me, feels warm and fuzzy. Maybe you pepper in some sage advice, so this never happens again. It made me feel good like I'd done a kind deed and changed a student's life.

I quickly figured out that Santa Clause wasn't just a mistake; it can be crippling for some students. First mistake: This was never about me and making me feel good. I had wrongly rationalized that giving students what they wanted may be the one break they needed; maybe it could turn around their academic careers. It was selfish of me to believe that. Second, what kind of message does this send to other students? Do you know how pissed off I would be if I were a student who worked my balls off for a good grade and then found out that someone who screwed off the whole semester still got a decent grade? It's still not about me, but what kind of reputation does this give me? Am I a pushover to dilute myself into thinking I'm a good and virtuous person? Maybe the break I give to a student who is drying their tears does turn them around, and they've learned their lesson. Or perhaps that same student continues bad academic habits because they realize they can talk themselves out of anything? I'm not willing to take that risk, ever. That's how it works in the real world.

I don't know the answer to the "immaturity" problem, but most universities do; I know mine does. A good university like mine recognizes that not all students have the same maturity level, and that's OK. I'm not a massive fan of corporate-speak, but I like one of our school sayings: "... measured not by whom it excludes, but by whom it includes and how they succeed." I believe it. People way more intelligent than me (and that's a lot of people!) have figured out different paths and custom programs to include all sorts of students to navigate a university successfully and get a great outcome. I lean on these "smarter" people for guidance and direction when dealing with specific students. Don't forget, boys and girls, maturity counts in college.

Do Mature Students Fail Too?

It's easy to understand why immature students fail, but what about mature students? Do they fail, too? Yep. Strangely enough, mature students take it harder than immature students who are used to failing. First-time failure in college can feel devastating when you have never had to deal with failure in high school. Remember, you were on the student council, in the National Honor Society, and took every AP class offered. Everything you did in high school worked; you were on cruise control. Fast forward to your first semester in college, and everyone in your dorm is talking about how hard that calculus midterm was and that half the class failed. That kind of news travels faster than any wildfire. Rumors of curving grades start to surface. Maybe you should have looked up the professor on RateMyProfessors.com before signing up for the class? Perhaps they'll drop your lowest exam score? Fact is, you failed, maybe for the first time. It's not the end of the world, even though it might feel that way.

If you're a first-year first-semester student who failed the first exam for lack of preparation, who's at fault? That's easy; it's my fault, for starters. It's my job to convey all expectations, including how to prepare and excel at all exams and assignments. I talk about exam prep in almost every class. It's so mind-numbingly repetitive that it makes students glaze over faster than talking about that time I went to a Bruce Springsteen concert when I was in college. Be that as it may, it's essential to prepare. Most educators and college provosts say you need to spend two hours preparing and studying outside the classroom for every hour you're in class. If you take a 15-hour course load, you should prepare and study for another 30 hours a week. That's 45 hours a week, more than most full-time jobs.

How you study and prepare is also crucial. First, let me dispel one of the stupidest sayings in history: Learn to multitask. It's wrong on so many levels. I'm sure it sounded good in a marketing brochure or some inspirational quote from a self-appointed expert on

LinkedIn, but multitasking is always wrong. Computers multitask; people don't. Instead, train yourself to focus on one subject at a time. Know what you're doing ahead of time. What chapters should you be reading? Do the practice problems. Important: If you can find great study partners, then do it! Remember, great study partners don't put up with shit. Don't be late, don't be the village idiot without anything to offer.

Remember, the university isn't high school. Keep in mind that some high schools depend on students to get the highest grades possible because it reflects well on the high school. Universities don't. Some high schools need you to get top grades because it bodes well for their overall rankings, potential future funding, and even administrative bonuses. Because of this, some high schools are willing to extend deadlines, bend the rules, hold your hand for four years, and spoon-feed you, which is not a sound formula for future university success. This is in no way an indictment of all high schools. Most are awesome. Most high school teachers are fantastic, and their jobs are infinitely more complex than mine.

Is Time Management a Big Deal?

Manage your time wisely. You might have heard of Jocko
Willink, a famous podcaster, keynote speaker, and former Navy
SEAL. One of his most memorable sayings is, "You don't need
motivation; you need discipline." Think about it; everything
motivates you in college: fear of failure, drive to succeed, your
parents, your friends, acclaim from others, potential high-paying
jobs. I could go on, but I think you get the point. Motivation in
college is a given. What you need is the discipline that will get you
through university successfully. The dictionary defines discipline as
"training to act by rules." The "training" part of the definition means
you must put in a lot of effort to stick to your rules. The good part is
that you make the rules.

Here's where you start: Your class schedule. It's the bedrock that
you build the rest of your university life around. If you had your shit
together in high school, you would have registered for your
university classes sometime during the middle of your senior year,
like mid-December to mid-January. It ensures the classes you want
at the times you want.

Pro tip: When you are at university, always take advantage of
pre-registration for the next semester immediately when courses
post. Nothing sucks more than a class at 8 a.m. on Thursday, a super
long break, and a 3 p.m. class the same day.

Start here for a solid time management plan: You need to
identify and define what to spend your time on. I'm not just talking
about class schedules and study time, either. Include fun stuff like
intramural sports and socializing and important stuff like eating and
sleeping well. Once you've done that, figure out what activities are
the most time-consuming and which are most important. You can
write all this down or choose from the infinite number of time
management apps.

Once you've included all activities, start seriously prioritizing
them. What's more important, your Tuesday/Thursday calculus class

or playing Halo on Xbox? Don't answer that. Make sure you differentiate between "most important task" and "most urgent task." Yep, something urgent will get in the way of the most important. Part of time management ensures that never happens. Once again, use an app so it harangues you with a "to-do" list. Learn to schedule your activities appropriately.

Next, consider Admiral William H. McRaven, who gave one of the most viral commencement speeches at his alma mater, the University of Texas. His speech outlined how he became successful and started with modest advice, "Make your bed." Try it. Type "make your bed" into YouTube, and thousands of videos will pop up because of the admiral's straightforward message: Start the day off by accomplishing an easy task, and organization will follow. McRaven points out that the little things in life matter. I'll never give a commencement speech, but I would say, "Get your shit together, don't be messy, pay attention to the little things, stay in a decent environment, and hang around good people. That's the best time management advice I can give.

Maybe the most challenging aspect of time management is knowing when you are wasting time. Remember what I said about being selfish and choosing yourself and studying over almost anything else? I get it; an iPhone with TikTok, Instagram, and a host of other distractions can feel like escapism, a small break from the rigors of university. Roommates that drop by unexpectedly can be a nice break from studying but put the brakes on when they impede your schedule by staying too long. Here's the bottom line: Get the time management app and stick to it. Deal?

Is it OK to Miss Class in College?

How many F-bombs can you drop before a PG e-book turns into an R-rated e-book? The answer is more than one. I am well past my limit in this rant, so I will restrain myself and say: Go to effing class! Never miss class, ever. The only reason to cut class is that you are sick or have a legitimate emergency.

Every fall in my vast lecture hall, when my classes are packed to the gills with first-semester first-year students, I ask a few questions on the very first day. I ask if there happens to be a sophomore, junior, or senior in the room. There invariably always are. Usually, they have changed majors and need to take my required core class and must suffer through a first-year course. All of them have seen at least a few semesters of university, so I ask them a straightforward question: What is the key to success at university? They all say the same thing: The secret to college is going to class, period. A common first-day question is whether I take attendance or not? Nope, I don't take attendance. I will never report you to the principal's office, and no one will call you out for skipping class. While I have the upper-level students' attention, I always ask them my next question on the first day of class: Do semesters go fast? Typical responses are: "Holy shit, oh my God, yes, way faster than you can imagine, hyper-fast, etc." I want first-semester, first-year students to hear it from students who have been there and not just from me.

Let me give you an idea of how fast semesters go. Most semesters, I attend my school's commencement ceremony (my school does it right, and it's super fun). I dress up in my Professor Snape outfit, a long flowing robe hotter than a sauna. I wear a goofy tasseled hat last in fashion during the early Renaissance. My Ray-Ban sunglasses are a must because the event is typically at night in a giant football stadium with floodlights pointed directly at my eyes. For the most part, I'm window-dressing sitting on stage and about as crucial as the potted plant next to me. But I get to do one of my favorite things: Thank students for being awesome. I get tons of handshakes and awkward hugs from graduating seniors that have been pre-gaming since 10 a.m. (Be careful, kids.) I get to hang around with thousands of graduates after the ceremony, and there's one common theme, "Holy shit, that went fast. It seems like yesterday I was a snot-nosed freshman sitting in your class." My not-so-subtle point is that you can't procrastinate at college. Semesters go lightning fast.

Are There People Trying to take Advantage of You on Campus?

Every spring, especially during an election year, you will run into a "Register to vote" guy hanging out in high-traffic areas of campus, clipboard in hand, asking anyone and everyone if they've registered to vote. You may feel like adulting and decide it's time to declare your political party affiliation proudly. Good for you! "Register to vote" guy gladly complies with your request by handing you a very official-looking document and letting you borrow his pen so you can fill out your name, address, city, state, ZIP code, phone number, and email. Oh, wait, one more thing, he'll need your signature, too. The problem is, he couldn't give a rat's ass whether you're registered to vote or not, he wants to steal your personal information, and you just gave it to him on a silver platter.

What about the "Do you have a minute for the environment" girl? Who doesn't want to save the baby seals? Of course, no one gives a shit about saving the south Atlantic brine shrimp, but baby seals are so adorable, and you don't want them to end up as warm baby seal mittens. "Do you have a minute for the environment" girl does the same thing as the "Register to vote" guy who stole your identity and privacy, but with one difference. She asks for a donation. After all, it takes money to keep baby seals safe from the evil mitten industry. You say you don't have cash, but that's OK. You have Venmo and Zelle, and by sheer coincidence, so does she! Do you see where this is going?

I had a student tell me that some guys on campus offered her a free trip to Las Vegas to do some modeling. There's a name for the guys who make offers like that; they're called predators. There are different kinds of predators, too. For example, there are nondenominational preachers in crowded areas who scream at you through a megaphone that you are a depraved whore, and they hold the secret to everlasting redemption. No kidding. It happens. There is never a shortage of students willing to get into shouting matches with these so-called evangelists and call them false prophets. Here's my advice, don't engage them. Just walk by with the comfort of knowing you're not a depraved whore. You're not a whore at all.

Is the 'Freshman 15' Real?

The "Freshman 15" is a myth; it's more like the Freshman 20. I am not kidding. The Freshman 15 says you'll gain 15 pounds your first year in college. The only reason it's not called the Freshman 20 is it doesn't rhyme, but it's more accurate. If there is one common thing on every campus, it's food. It's not unusual for a Starbucks or Burger King to be part of a university's food service contract. I'm not saying those are bad foods, but too much is. Sure, there are many healthy options on campus, but no one eats raisins and celery as comfort food when they're homesick unless Ranch dressing or peanut butter covers them. Access to food on campus is as easy as using an app where a robot can deliver a can of Pringles (poor packaging but delicious) and a quart of cookies and cream ice cream. (That's a real thing.) Do I even have to make a point here? Exercise regularly and eat well. (See the chapter *Is Time Management a Big Deal.*)

There's a reason everyone is wearing saggy sweats toward the end of the semester. Remember those amenities I mentioned, specifically student recreation centers and dining halls? Remember that thing I said about managing your time? Do I need to tell you what you already know? Eat stuff that's good for you and exercise regularly. (Again, see the chapter *Is Time Management a Big Deal.*) Donuts are evil.

Why Aren't You Sitting in the Front of the Class?

Here's a reason *not* to sit in the front of the class: the intimidation factor. The professor asks some dreadfully impossible questions, and there you are, upfront, every student behind you is looking at the hairs standing on the back of your neck because you don't know the answer. No one else in the class knows the answer, but the professor will call on you because you're convenient and in front. That's your theory anyway, so you avoid the front of the classroom like the plague.

Professors generally give their attention to the front and the back of the classroom. It's almost like the middle of the classroom is being subtly ignored. Hell, maybe that's how you want the professor to treat you in class, with an unconscious, sort of mild neglect. You're somewhat shy and retiring, so you opt for the middle of the classroom, a much worse place for you.

OK, it's settled. You should sit in the back, which is the worst place for any student. It's the most distracting part of the classroom where it's too easy to look around, daydream, clock-watch, and observe other students who still don't know the answer. Perfect, that means there's nowhere to sit if you're shy and retiring. The front is too scary, the middle gets neglected, and the back is too distracting.

I'm on your side. Let's agree that all options are equally bad for you if you're shy. Sit in the front anyway, off to the side if it makes you feel better. There are mountains of research indicating that students who sit up front are more likely to do well in class. The problem with that research is that it seems suspect because it ignores all the go-getters, ass kissers, and hyper-motivated students who are already sitting there. Believe it or not, significant research places sample groups randomly in a classroom setting. It indicates that the students who sit upfront will still do the best, regardless of personality traits. Look, at least give it a try. Start slow, sit up front in your least intimidating favorite class, or gradually work your way up to the front during the semester. Sitting in the front of a classroom for better grades is a real thing, promise.

Is it Safe on a College Campus?

I was never in a frat because I couldn't afford the dues. I only owned service station shirts that smelled like body odor and gasoline, and I was too old to be a frat boy when I came back to college. I suppose I had unfair, preconceived notions about frat guys, but let me tell you what, boys and girls, they saved my ass regularly when I used to teach night classes. One night in class, a couple of well-dressed, well-spoken young men approached me before my lecture and said they were with SAE. (Sigma Alpha Epsilon, I think.) They said they escorted anyone back to their dorms or dark parking structures as part of their voluntary community service and ensured they got in their car safely. They made sure whomever they were escorting was safe. That was their mission. They asked if I could announce to my night class that they were waiting outside the classroom doors if anyone needed their services. I gladly did, and many people took them up on their offer.

Universities typically have a more well-structured service than those SAE boys, making sure no one walks alone, especially at night on a vast campus. Call them or use their app, and they will be there in minutes. They even offer to give you a ride in their fancy golf carts, especially if you sprained your ankle and have mobility issues. You don't need to do a walk of shame at 3 a.m. Campus security and personal safety are the highest priorities for all universities. For the most part, university campuses are safe. The university, university police, frat boys, etc., do everything to keep it that way.

Last thing: Treat an empty, dark college campus like an empty, dark city. (See the chapter Nothing Good Happens After Midnight.) Be safe, be vigilant.

Should You Reboot When You Arrive on Campus?

One of my biggest regrets in college is that I never took advantage of the reboots as an Air Force brat. Let me explain. My dad was a combat fighter pilot in the Air Force, so we moved around. By the time I'd finished my master's degree, I had been to 17 different schools. You might think it was hard to make new friends every move, but since the other kid's parents at the new location were flight nurses, tank commanders, or postmaster generals, they moved around a lot as well, and we all knew the drill. But here's the thing: Making new friends every year and a half was like rebooting my computer and starting fresh, just like going to college. It was an opportunity to be a better version of myself because my new friends at the new location didn't have any preconceived notions of who I was.

I regret never rebooting as a better version of myself for college and searching out people who wouldn't just be friends but people who would benefit me in my pursuit of a degree. Dan Pena, the infamous, foul-mouthed billionaire, has a saying that goes something like this, "Show me your friends, and I will show you your future." That's doubly true in a university setting. Are your friends potheads, Adderall dealers, or losers going nowhere fast? Then you are, too. They're probably going to flunk out and drag you down with them. Even though universities can be huge, you'd be surprised at how quickly you can get a bad reputation. For example, take group work in college. No one likes it. There's no way around it, but there it is. Another saying also applies nicely, "If you're in a group and can't figure out who's the village idiot, it's probably you."

Don't be that guy. Give the reboot a try when you arrive on campus.

Do You Need to Make Friends the Day You Arrive on Campus?

Y ou don't need to make friends the second you arrive on campus. I'm not saying to be unfriendly. Just pace yourself. Go to social events, check out the gym, join a co-ed ultimate frisbee team, or sign up for an intramural quidditch team (seriously, that's a thing.) The activities on a college campus are endless, typically free (OK, tuition and ongoing fees cover them), run day and night, and are listed on your school's website. Avoid bad-energy people (trust your instincts) and start getting your head around a problematic concept you might not have learned at home: Be selfish in pursuing your degree. I'm not saying you're not caring and charitable. When choosing between you and anything that gets in the way of your degree, choose you. For instance, I know you're a good listener and a good person, but do you need to comfort someone crying all night about their recent breakup for hours on end when it's keeping you up too late or keeping you from class? That might make you feel like a virtuous person in the short run, but your time might be the most precious commodity you have at university.

Don't be an island, either. I know you're better. Friends happen, but don't force it. The first few days on a college campus can seem confusing and lonely, so you might catch yourself impatient to make friends, leading to mistakes. Do you want to play video games all night with your new friends just not to be alone? Stay busy when you start. There's no shame in calling mom or dad. They'll be over the moon (and probably keep you on that FaceTime call longer than you want).

Should You Start a Study Group?

Y ou may not appreciate this right away, but your study group partners may be better than your friends. They will probably become your friends anyway, so hear me out. First, how do you find a study group? You can go online to specific group chats on your school's discussion boards or use free apps like My Study Life, but the best study groups are live and in person. The best way to start a study group is to ask other students in class. It's not a cheesy pickup line, either. Here is a subtle technique when talking to students in your class: "I'm trying to get in a study group for this class. Do you guys know of any?" What if someone says, "Yes?" Perfect. What if they say "No?" Then say you'd like to start one, and would any of you be interested? The next step: Don't get the phone numbers of potential study group partners right away. (No Snapchat either — that's very different.) Keep it to emails.

Once you get your study group up and going, there are some hard and fast rules. Answer study group emails promptly! Never meet at a private location. Make sure it always feels super safe for the entire group. Never meet in someone's dorm room for study groups. Your weird roommate won't appreciate the distraction, and they think you're weird, too. Meet in public places like the library. Never, ever miss a study group meeting unless you absolutely must. Make sure you give your team advanced notice if you must miss — schedule study group meetings way ahead of time (see the chapter *Is Time Management a Big Deal*). Don't be a sponge, be a valuable member of your team. Bring your snacks and chew with your mouth closed. Make rules that work for everyone.

Everyone agrees that meeting for class on Zoom during the Covid pandemic sucked in almost every conceivable way, whether you were an instructor or student. Still, the worst part was the lack of live human collaboration and interaction as far as I am concerned. Collaborating with other students is one of your most significant resources in college. And yes, you might get a friend or two out of the deal. Just stop chewing with your mouth open.

Nothing Good Happens After Midnight

It would be disingenuous not to include my take on college parties.
Most gatherings typically start after 10 p.m. regardless of the day of
the week, and Thursday nights are a famous kickoff to the weekend.
Most parties will include alcohol and drugs (weed, Adderall, and
Rohypnol are popular.) Bragging that your school is the "No. 1"
party school in the nation is equivalent to saying your school loses
more students to drugs, alcohol, and suicide than any other school in
the country. College parties can have a very dark side with real
consequences: drug overdoses; sexual assaults; arrests; blackouts;
driving under the influence; Rohypnol abuse, aka "roofies," the date
rape drug; and too many more dire consequences to list.

You're mistaken if you think your university isn't paying
attention. I've heard of students being kicked out of dorms in the first
week of school because the university saw an airplane-sized bottle of
Jack Daniels and red solo cups in their dorm room on social media.
Yes, that happens. I have had university police interrupt my class
asking if anyone knows the whereabouts of a particular student, only
to find they had died drunk and alone days earlier. Universities have
a "zero tolerance" approach to alcohol and drugs, as they should. Did
you know potential employers do deep forensic dives into your
social media accounts? It doesn't matter if you deleted your
Facebook, Instagram, Snap Chat, or TikTok accounts. Those not-so-
flattering images are still out there, trust me. So, is college partying
that involves drugs or alcohol worth the risk? My answer is a big,
"Hell, no!"

If Darth Vader ever met you, he might say, "The FOMO is
strong in this one. Resistance to alcohol and drug-fueled college
parties is futile." The peer pressure is so overwhelming that it's
palpable; you'll lose social capital and friends if you don't go to
college parties and drink. You might hear your mom, "If your friends
jumped off a bridge, would you jump, too?" But you're unsupervised
for the first time. The party is in Chad's room, who lives in your

dorm, and you know him. What's the big deal if you get drunk? It's only beer, and it's free. Even if you pass out, you never leave the building.

I'm sitting here staring at the screenwriting about college partying, wondering how dark I should go. Is it way too dark or an essential PSA about the potential realities of college parties? I know that I'm not your mom. I hold zero sway over your decision-making, so I will end this topic with this next part. Warning: The next part of this paragraph is very dark and NSFW (not safe or suitable for work.) Think about this scenario, regardless of your gender: Someone sexually assaulted you in the early morning after blacking out at a college party. You're defenseless, super dizzy, and have no idea whose room you're in at the dorm. Now what? Go to university police? Maybe go to the campus health center? How about calling your mom or dad, whom you lied to hours earlier that you would be with friends at the library? What about saying nothing to anyone, ever, because you're not sure who assaulted you? But you have to say something because the predator is still at large, right? Did you pick up a sexually transmitted disease? The real fun begins when you start blowing up all over social media.

Do I still think you're going to end up at a college party involving drugs and alcohol? Yes, I do. I'm not an idiot. In an article for ScholarshipPoints.com, Michelle Adams shares common-sense ways to protect yourself, starting with this:

- **Know your limits**. That's a big ask for some first-time drinkers. How the hell would they know their limits without experimentation? It's excellent advice.
- **Stick with your friends**. There is safety in numbers.
- **Get a safety app**. There are many options, and they're accessible and work. These apps can tell whether you're sober or drunk, reminding you to cool it if you can't walk straight. More importantly, it lets friends know where you are and if you're in an unsafe environment.
- **Always keep an eye on your drink**. If you lost track of your drink, pour it out.
- **Designate a driver**. Make sure someone takes one for the team.

- **Protect your privacy**, and don't post your drunken selfies on social media. Predators depend on drunken social media posts, and Big Brother is always watching.

Take Time for Yourself

The first chair of my department (my first boss at university) was an accomplished scholar, a skilled educator, and an even better person. He's the guy that hired me (at the deli) and took me under his wing when he didn't have to. After he retired, I missed him because he had an open-door policy and was always willing to answer questions or just shoot the shit. During my first semester, very late at night, he caught me in my office sorting through 800 exam papers I needed to get into alphabetical order. There was paper everywhere, on my desk, floor, and shelves. I figured I had hours more to finish when he found me. He was at the campus late for some random university function and decided to grab something from his office before heading home. He was towering over me as I sat on my office floor covered with paper. He said something I've never forgotten, **"Go home**." He didn't ask what I was doing or if what I was doing was necessary, or even why. He could have cared less. I started to explain myself, but he still could not have possibly cared less and repeated, "Go home."

He gave me the best advice I have ever gotten at the university on the way out the door. He said, "This place will eat you alive if you keep up these hours. You need to be away from this university now and then. I don't want to see you here during winter break either, and I don't want you thinking about this place while you're gone. You need to take time for yourself." Thanks, Bob. That advice was from over 20 years ago, and it still holds today. I pass along this advice on the first day to students in the hundreds of classes I have taught on the first day because it's that important. Make time to be away from your university and don't even think about it, even if it's for a few fleeting hours. Do something else, do anything else. Be selfish, even if it's against your nature, but do it for yourself. Taking time for yourself might be the best advice I can pass on other than never to miss Taco Tuesdays.

Should You Join a College Club?

Let me start with academic and professional clubs, especially within your majors like the Economics Club or the Future Teachers Club. Giant employers from all over the country come to schools to present dusty PowerPoint presentations professionally crafted by some unhappy soul in their marketing department to show them at universities to professional student clubs. Professional club meetings like these happen on campus every night of the week in any given semester. Companies typically start by telling you that Angus someone or other started Consolidated Dust Inc. sometime before the bronze age while providing a brief history of their illustrious organization. As a faculty director of many campus clubs, I've seen a few of these presentations devolve into mind-numbing nightmares. But most organizations make their companies look so damn tempting to work for that most students are ready to sign up then and there. Some better organizations even bring your school's alumni employees to speak, which is an incredibly devious and effective ploy.

When I started as a faculty director of a few professional student clubs, I convinced myself that these companies were doing us a huge solid. Many of them fly in from other parts of the country to speak to our professional clubs. They even buy the hundred or so club members in attendance Pizza and Diet Coke. (OK, they're expensing it, but that's not the point.) Being the knucklehead I am, I finally figured out we were doing them a favor. They were here to recruit our students and give them a taste of what it looks like if you work for them as a full-time employee after graduation or as a paid summer intern.

Organizations want to meet our students in a more personal, face-to-face setting that professional clubs afford instead of a busy career fair held in a Costco-sized room where they collect 30,000 paper resumes. The student organizers, typically juniors or seniors, know the organizations that come to see them. The club's officers never invite the mind-numbing companies back and exclusively ask those who give internships and hire our graduates. So yes, academic clubs are worth it.

Universities do something wise when it comes to social clubs. They ask social clubs to register with the university and sanction them. Let's say you want to start a drone racing club on your campus. Universities will require you to write up and adopt bylaws for your potential club, fill out what seems like an endless pile of paperwork, and jump through flaming hoops. At first blush, it looks like a giant pain in the ass, but there's a good reason for it. They need to know that any clubs are legitimate (for liability purposes). They ensure clubs are safe for students before they're willing to sanction and list them on the school's website. Yes, they will require a faculty representative and status reports every semester. Because the university has vetted the club, you can confirm these clubs are legit. Just pick one or two from the hundreds of student organizations. Club interests on any given campus are seemingly infinite and worth it.

Back when I was in college and dirt was new, if you wanted to be the BMOC (Big Man on Campus for the youngsters), you had an Intramural Champions T-shirt and proudly wore it until it was completely tattered. These T-shirts represented that you were the pinnacle of athletic achievement, and you probably could have gone to the Olympics or played pro ball; at least, that's how they made you feel. Great universities like mine have full-time staff whose sole purpose is to set up and administer every conceivable intramural sport at any level. I was astonished (but not surprised) when my daughter (BWOC) came home from college wearing an Intramural Champions T-shirt for co-ed flag football. (The one that should have been point guard.) She had the same feeling about that T-shirt that I did many years ago. College intramurals and club sports are worth it. Do it. (See the *Take Time for Yourself* chapter.)

Should You Take Advantage of Summer School at Community College?

Remember when I told you about how effing fantastic community colleges are? I was dead serious. But first, bear with me as I go on a rant about math before telling you where community college comes to the rescue.

If you're like me, you detest math with a fiery passion and are confident math hates you back. You can't reconcile why college requires math, let alone high school. You know math will be of no use later in life. You actively advocate for its abolition in college whenever it comes up in conversation, especially in math classes when the problems mix in alphabetic letters and Greek characters with good old-fashioned numbers. But you know that all your bitching and moaning will fall on deaf ears, and, what's worse, you're still going to have to take a required math class or two to complete your degree. Your precious GPA (calculated with stupid math) will suffer because someone thought it was essential to calculate the arc cosine of an obtuse circle thingy. I wasn't paying attention.

So, where does community college enter when it comes to math? If you have unhinged, unfounded, and irrational fear of any subject and are willing to spread ignorant opinions like me, why not take that subject at the local community college in the summer if it's a first- or second-year student-level class? Remember I told you community college professors are fantastic. I wasn't kidding. Would you prefer a smaller, less stressful setting that only lasts six to eight weeks? Remember the low cost of tuition part of community colleges? How about the aspect of GPA not transferring over to your four-year university? How about the equivalency part? (Make sure the community college course is equivalent and counts toward your four-year university degree beforehand.) Remember that, too?

OK, hear me out: I've known plenty of people who planned their four-year university classes and major maps way ahead of time by including equivalent summer community college classes, whether they loathed math. Some did it because they wanted to be a full-time student but only take 12 hours (maybe they have jobs) instead of 15, reducing stress for their first few semesters in college. Many people use community college for the convenience of a shorter semester where they might kiss and make up with math and come to understand that math loved them the whole time.

Should You Take any Self-Paced or Online Classes?

Self-paced? No. Online? Maybe. (Especially if you're a first-semester first-year student.) Research I read in an academic journal that I can't remember the name of (trust me) indicates that self-paced classes are only viable and successful for adult learners. I remember the research because it said you had to be 37 years old or older, and I thought that was such an oddly specific number. What if you're only 36? It went on to say self-paced classes only worked if the student was paying for the course out of their pocket. Self-paced courses in my business school are not offered as an option since they're frowned upon, especially for first- and second-year students. I know what you're thinking; I'll stick to my time management plan and be motivated and disciplined. Please stop it. Listen to me; you'll ghost that self-paced class faster than that disastrous date who showed up 20 minutes late, didn't pay for the meal, and brought their mom. Avoid self-paced at all costs.

When it comes to online classes, they are not all created equal. I've taken poorly structured, crappy online courses from a simple website homepage with a university logo. The lessons consisted of copy instructing me to read the book, do the assignments at the back of the chapters, and turn my work into a professor whose name is loosely associated with the course and who doesn't respond to emails except for Tuesday nights after "Jeopardy!" That doesn't feel a whole lot different than self-paced. Some poorly constructed online classes can make you feel alone on an island because there's no direct contact with the instructor and, more importantly, your classmates.

There are many misconceptions about quality online classes. For example, online courses are more manageable than their traditional classroom counterparts. That's invalid. Another misconception is that the learning outcome isn't as good in an online setting, which is also not true. Somehow, online classes have also gotten the reputation that you won't have to spend as much time as you would in a traditional classroom. That is not true either. Here's the deal, when a good university offers any online class, they go through the same rigorous scrutiny and audit process as their in-class counterparts, and for important reasons, namely offering quality learning options and protecting and keeping their accreditation. It's in their best interest to ensure their online and in-class courses are essentially the same other than the platform.

Why Would You Take Online Classes?

Let's start here: Can you take online classes full-time and get a four-year university degree without ever setting foot on a campus or even being in the same state? The answer amazingly is yes; it happens all the time. To be clear, staying exclusively online for a degree is not an alternative from a university standpoint; it's simply a different learning platform. I know that sounds like a technicality, but it's not; most universities offer an infinite array of complete degree programs with the same instructors, advisors, books, major maps, assignment deadlines, etc. The only real difference is that one is online and the other in a classroom.

The apparent benefits of online learning are that you don't have to be in a specific place at a particular time, there's no long commute, it works around your schedule, and you can complete your degree in your pajamas. However, I have seen some of my students wearing pajamas in my class, usually late in the semester. That being the case, it doesn't necessarily mean the online school is less expensive, less rigorous, or more accessible. Expect to work hard and independently sometimes. Yes, you will have classmates, but you'll have to work harder to develop relationships with other students for group projects and form effective study groups.

Here is an awkward question prospective students want to know, but they're too afraid to ask about full-time online universities: What will my diploma say? Will those big, beautiful gothic letters on my certificate say **Big State *Online* University**, or will it be like everyone else's diploma and say **Big State University**? The answer is that it will say "Big State University" because the outcome for full-time online students is considered the equivalent of an on-campus student's experience in the physical classroom. Universities don't differentiate between brick-and-mortar buildings and cyberspace; it's their way of offering more options to pursue a college degree.

What if you're a first-semester first-year student ready to enjoy the college experience and have no interest in a full-time online university? Then the question is: Are a few online classes peppered in with your full-time in-person courses a good idea? Online courses can feel self-paced, but I assure you they're not. It's also easy to put off the coursework for online classes. Yes, online classes can supplement your in-person courses. However, let's say you have 12 credit hours of in-class courses and three credit hours in an online setting for 15 credit hours total. Be sure this schedule still qualifies you as a full-time student. You may think you're taking pressure off your academic program because you only have 12 in-class credit hours. You are not. That three-hour online class will take as much time as any in-class course. With all this in mind, take an online class because it's convenient and not because you think it will be easier.

Super-secret pro tip: Here's an online class pro tip I hesitate to give, but a typical university has more than one semester going during the fall. When the fall semester starts, there's a traditional 16-week semester and another more intensive eight-week online semester running concurrently, and they both begin simultaneously. After the first eight-week online semester is over, another eight-week online semester begins, ending simultaneously with the 16-week semester. Got all that? OK, let's say you are entirely bombing a class, and you have no one to blame but yourself while taking a traditional 16-week in-class course. Let's also say you realize you're flunking out sometime around week seven. Sure, maybe dig in and possibly squeak out a D or a C, but consider this: Withdraw (drop) from the 16-week class you're flunking at the seven-week mark and sign up for the same class given in the second eight-week online semester. Think about it. You already have a pretty good idea of what the course is about, you already bought the book, and now you have a second chance to redeem yourself and get an A with no messy explanation to mom or dad during the winter break.

Note: Online classes usually have fees associated with them, so it might cost $50 to $100 when making the switch.

What Happens if You Drop a Class?

Dropping a class or withdrawing, as it's sometimes called, can be a bit tricky for many reasons. Maybe you think you will fail a class or get a bad grade and don't want it reflected on your transcripts, pulling down your GPA. Perhaps you're overwhelmed, and you want to reduce your course load. Maybe you've decided you aren't all that interested in the history of the Kardashians; it's not an easy "A," and you did poorly on the Khloé quiz.

The first thing to consider when dropping a class is whether it will put you behind schedule for your major. Maybe the course you're considering dropping, English 101, is a prerequisite for English 102, which you need down the road. If you drop English 101 in the fall semester, you'll have to take it in the spring semester, and then English 102 gets pushed back to the next semester. Dropping classes can have a natural domino effect on graduating on time. Universities publish course withdrawal deadlines on their academic calendars detailing the last day you are allowed to drop and whether you'll get a potential refund. Be aware of these dates before you start university.

Another thing to consider when dropping a class is whether it affects your status as a full-time student. For instance, 15 hours is a typical course load at the school where I work and is considered "full-time." The minimum number of hours is 12, regarded as a full-time student and essential for many reasons. What if you have a 12-hour course load and decide to drop a class that lowers you to a nine-hour course load? You won't be a full-time student, and you might lose services on campus, such as the university healthcare system, access to the student recreation center, etc. Understand what constitutes a full-time student at your university and what advantages it brings before you withdraw from a class.

Some people treat a "W" on their transcript as though it's a scarlet letter. (Remember that book you were supposed to read in high school?) Some see it as a failure and a black mark and wonder if future employers who see their transcripts will think so, too. That may be true if you have a long history of "Ws" scattered throughout seven years of school, like the star character in the movie "Tommy Boy," Thomas R. Callahan III, a graduate of Marquette University. Still, in my opinion, a couple of "Ws" won't be that big of a deal, especially if you're thoughtful before applying for a job. (Besides, Mr. Callahan had a job waiting for him after college.)

Are Student-Athletes Good Students?

Student-athletes are an impressive bunch, and that's after seeing hundreds of them in my classes for more than two decades. (I had the distinct honor of meeting Pat Tillman, the epitome of the student-athlete, and he was every bit as impressive as you've heard.) No one becomes a college athlete by accident. They get there with drive and discipline, sticking to schedules, the same things it takes to be a phenomenal student. It makes no difference if they're on the football team or the sand volleyball team. Universities don't give out scholarships, housing, food, etc., lightly. Universities are aware that student-athletes represent the school and brand in almost every conceivable way, and they will do almost anything to ensure the image doesn't get tarnished. To guarantee the school image isn't tainted, they ensure their potential student-athletes have the same discipline in their athletics as in the classroom. The term "student-athlete" is not by accident. Athletes are students first.

Don't believe me? Since my classes have thousands of students that include many student-athletes every semester, I get invited by my student-athletes to almost every sport the university offers, from water polo to volleyball. It's not unusual for the average athletic department's student-athletes to have a GPA above 3.4, and, yes, this includes football players. For the most part, student-athletes are typically excellent examples to follow.

Do Excuses Work in College?

Why doesn't the news media cover the **Grampocalypse**? As far as I can figure out, it happens four times a year, so you would think it would draw more national media attention. I'm not an acclaimed research scientist, but the best I can correlate is that tens of thousands of grandmas and grandpas pass away like clockwork just before fall and spring college midterms and final exams. Every semester, the **Grandemic** seems to show up at the most inopportune time, denying students the chance to study for and take the midterm and final exams they couldn't wait to take.

You have my sincere and deepest condolences, seriously. I am genuinely sorry and empathetic about your loss and will do anything and everything I can to get you back on track when you're ready to come back to school. However, a tiny percentage of the Grandemic is bogus and made-up excuses to get out of assignments or exams. I know that's almost impossible to believe, but I have seen it happen. True story: I had a student go so far as to make up fake holy cards with Photoshop for the passing of their grandma. One of my more hardnosed graduate assistants pointed out that the dates were three years earlier, and grandma lived the high life in Santa Barbara, California.

The overwhelming majority of excuses I get are not excuses; they are legitimate reasons a student can't attend class. Not only that, but these students are also more than willing to provide honest documentation and the specific dates they will be away from class. Student-athletes are especially good at letting professors know when they will be gone, where they will be, and when they will return. It is for these students I would be happy to accommodate in any way.

Unfortunately, since a small minority of students have abused the "excuse" system, most professors will require documentation from everyone. It always feels crass to ask the honest student for copies of a death certificate, doctor's note, or airline ticket, but please blame those who abuse the system.

There are a few small tricks professors do to verify excuses other than documentation. One is to check the email trail of a suspected repeat offender whose grandma has miraculously died multiple times during the semester. Another way professors vet repeat offenders is by looking at their previous grades throughout the semester. Suppose there is a pattern of missed assignments and low exam scores, and their emails contain various excuses throughout the semester. In that case, professors are less inclined to believe the story's integrity. Now and again, I get an email from a student who says they will miss a week mid-semester because their dad planned a family trip during this time. Sometimes someone can't miss their sister's mid-semester wedding. My first inclination is to wish the student a fun time in Cancun and hope everything works out between their sister and that guy the parents don't want her to marry. If you choose not to attend class for one of these reasons or another, I also assume you understand the potential consequences like missed learning opportunities, late penalties, etc. You wouldn't bail out of your job and disappear for a week and then act surprised when your employer fires you. You committed to your job the same way you engaged with the university. I'm not questioning your commitments or priorities; those are entirely up to you, but make the university a top priority, and don't make excuses, please.

Should You Fear Finals Week?

Y ou show up in room 714 in the science building 10 minutes ahead of time for your Wednesday Geology 101 class at 11 a.m. during finals week to take your final exam; that can be the difference between getting an A or a B for your semester grade. You plan to sit in the seat you've been sitting in the whole semester. Good news: You're the first to arrive, so you sit where you want. Then 15 minutes pass, then 20, and no one shows up, not even the instructor. You panic and step outside to recheck the door to see if you're in room 714, where you've been attending all semester long. You are in room 714. Where is everybody? You check the syllabus in a panic.

Important note: The final exam for Geology 101 will be given on the first Tuesday of the last week of classes at 8 p.m. in the engineering building.

How in the world could this have possibly happened? How did you miss this? That A you were banking on to bolster your GPA may have just turned into a D. Will you still be able to take the final exam?

Here's what happened: Some professors give a common final because they teach the same course five times a week. Rather than provide each class section a final exam, they find a room on campus big enough for all five sections of their classes to fit at once and give one big common final. For them, it's not only convenient, but the final exam questions don't spread all over campus and dorms like wildfire if they'd decided to give finals to their classes separately. Common finals are way easier to administer and proctor. Unfortunately, I have heard of unbending professors not willing to let wayward students take their final exams they missed because they were in the wrong place at the wrong time or just plain forgot. I've even heard of professors not letting students take final exams even if they were five minutes late; it's heartbreaking. (I'm not one of those guys, but I will be pissed if you miss my final exam.)

Know where you're supposed to be and when you're supposed to be there for final exams. Taking a final in a different room in a separate building on another day is not unusual at university. I know you've heard this 10 zillion times: Read the syllabus! (In the Army, they call it RTFM — read the fucking manual.) Would it be worse to check with the professor on where and when she'll give the final exam immediately after she said it to the class? Or would you rather miss the final exam because you didn't know where you were supposed to be, earning a D in a class you never missed and busted your ass to pass?

Pro tip: When scheduling your next semester's classes, determine when and where the final will be for each course. You can avoid final exams given on the last day of the final week and get home earlier.

What if You Just Plain Suck at Exams?

All this exam advice is well and good, but perhaps exams scare the shit out of you and make you anxious. You lose sleep the night before an exam because you're a nervous wreck. You're too scared to eat anything worthwhile before exams. You can't even poop. You lose focus in a room full of people who look like they could do the exam with their eyes closed, making you even more anxious. Your anxiety goes through the roof when other students start turning in their exams before you're halfway through with yours. It's not like you don't prepare well and study your ass off, but you feel like you'd do better if you took the exam alone in a more intimate setting. When you're in a room of 400 other students, it can feel like you're taking the exam in the middle of a busy Los Angeles freeway, especially when noisy students are in line searching for IDs, turning in completed Scantron exams to proctors.

If taking an exam simply proves to the instructor that you've retained and learned the course's information and have been heavily engaged all semester, isn't there an alternative way to take the exam? You don't want to be unfair to your classmates, but would it be too much to ask if you could have some extra time? How about if you could take the exam in a more private and less stressful setting? You can. Universities recognize that exams and quizzes can be overly stressful and have planned for this for students who qualify. Check into your university's testing services resource center if this sounds like you. I promise you'll be happy you did.

What are the Best Study Tips I've Ever Heard?

W hat follows is weird but stay with me. I knew a professor who suggested letting my students write absolutely anything they wanted on a four-by-six index card (both sides) and using it during an exam. I immediately snapped back and said there was no effing way I would do that. The problem was that I liked and respected this professor, so I took a considerable risk and tried it. You'd be amazed how small students can write; I needed an electron microscope to see some of their handwriting on their four-by-six index cards. Everyone is happy, and exam scores skyrocket. No shit, Sherlock! What did you think would happen? But I was still skeptical.

After I got all the exams from the students, my professor buddy encouraged me to ask them two specific questions. First, ask them if they liked using the four-by-six index cards? I got an overwhelming reaction, even applause. No shit! What did you think they were going to say? Second, and most importantly, I asked how often they referred to their four-by-six index card while taking the exam. I was floored by the response, as were the students. The room went quiet, which is unusual for 400 first-semester first-year students. The students told me they couldn't remember using the four-by-six index cards while taking the exam. Almost every student said they never looked at the four-by-six index card once while taking the exam, even after carefully preparing them.

What's the moral of the four-by-six index card caper? My professor buddy told me that he had read in some Harvard publication that writing stuff down is far more effective for knowledge retention than typing the same notes on a laptop with a keyboard. He wanted to experiment with my class to see if it was true. The fact is, I found out that writing stuff down is indeed more effective than typing it with a keyboard. I called him a butthole for

95

manipulating me, and he said, "You're welcome." Writing stuff down is good, even if you want to type it on your laptop later.

Pro tip: Understand that getting good sleep during a typical semester is at a premium, especially in a noisy dorm. You need to get a good night's sleep before taking your final exam, or any exam, and I mean eight hours or more in a row. (Catnaps here and there don't count.) I know that's a big ask in college but figure it out. Eat well before exams, too, and make sure it's food that's good for you, that fuels your brain. Last thing: Slow down during an exam but not too slow, maybe just 4 or 5% slower. Take your time to read the exam instructions. Read the whole exam before you begin.

What Happens When You Cheat in College?

To be clear, don't cheat in college — ever! I'm not a complete knucklehead, so I recognize the opportunities and temptations to cheat in college. I also understand the old saying, "If you cheat, you're only cheating yourself," which is about as effective as saying, "Just say no," so I will spare you a morality lecture. Instead, I'd advise you to start by understanding what constitutes cheating at university.

Any professor worth their salt will clearly outline their definition of what they and their university consider cheating. Of course, the professor will address cheating in their syllabi, but good professors will also address cheating and its consequences on the first day of class, and those consequences can be dire and long-lasting. Promise, I'm not playing Scared Straight — the juvenile awareness program that began in New Jersey in the 1970s — to discourage you from cheating, and you know I'm not your mom. You're at university now, but please consider the following few paragraphs.

Remember in middle school when your teacher threatened you that cheating on a quiz would go on your permanent record as a deterrent? As harmless as that threat was, universities don't threaten. Instead, they have made the "permanent record" a reality.

Let me cut to the chase with an example. Let's say you get caught cheating at the end of your sophomore year, halfway through your college career. You get called to the dean of discipline's office to plead your case, typically with no legal representation or parents; you're on your own. The verdict is guilty. There may be no appeal process if you are found guilty. Depending on the scenario and circumstances, many sentences are possible; maybe you get a zero on an assignment, a zero on the class's midterm examination, a zero for the semester and fail the course, or perhaps you get thrown out of school altogether. Regardless of the verdict, it's on your school record and sometimes on your transcripts, often required for grad school or future employment. Maybe you decide you'll take the 60 or so hours you've amassed and transfer to another university. You're going to need your transcripts to transfer, the one that says your last university kicked you out for cheating.

So, are you scared straight yet? Are you deterred now? That's not my intention. What's the lesson? Don't cheat in college because getting caught sucks? No, don't cheat because it's stupid, and it makes you stupid. Cheating on quizzes by employing apps offered by web-based scavengers has an actual and adverse effect. You can see the impact in a student's grades; perfect quiz scores all semester with failed midterms and final exams. Students go a whole semester memorizing quiz answers perfectly and then dump their important exams when they count. There are no majors in memorization. Please don't cheat in college.

The Worst College Advice I Ever Gave

Although I mainly focus on teaching first-semester core first-year classes, I sometimes get the opportunity to teach senior-level classes (usually advanced database design theory). As I have mentioned, seniors are different from first-year students; they didn't make it this far by accident; they've busted their collective asses. Toward the end of my database class one spring semester, one of the seniors named Rex (a tall, handsome redhead kid with a wry sense of humor who was an absolute pleasure to have in class) asked if I would attend commencement. All the seniors in class would be there with their moms and dads in tow, and I assured them I would be there dressed in my Snape costume. Then Rex asked if I had gone to my graduation ceremony so many years earlier. I told him I didn't attend my undergraduate commencement, but I did dress up and go to my graduate degree ceremony.

My students wanted to know what my graduate school commencement ceremony entailed. "Did you go hard on your pregame routine?" I told them that such a distinguished scholar as myself with a pristine reputation would never think of disrespecting such a venerated ritual as my university's articulation and commencement by sullying it with the devil's drink. They laughed at my bald-faced lie.

Rex said, "So, no funny business, no shenanigans, nothing cool happened at your commencement?" I said a few weird things happened, and something funny happened, but nothing of note. Rex asked, "Like what?" I told him I gave away my honor cords and Beta Gamma Sigma sash that hung around my neck on my Snape costume. A friend had earned the same honors as me, but her cords and sash never showed up in the mail, which had her in tears. She gave me a tearful hug after I put my cords and sash around her neck, and all was right with the world. I didn't care about that stuff; I was happy and amazed to be there. Rex said, "You are Santa Clause, and that's an awesome humblebrag, but it wasn't all that funny."

I told Rex, "I will tell you what I did that was funny but promise me you won't do what I did this weekend at your commencement. Deal? I'm serious, Rex!" Rex agreed. So, I started telling the whole class what had happened. As I was milling around a few minutes before we went up on stage to get our diplomas and hoods, I was standing around with a couple of friends I had been pregaming with a few hours earlier. Two of my buddies, both coincidently named Abdullah with different surnames, asked me why they were supposed to hand a card with their name on it to some decrepit old guy wearing a Dumbledore outfit on stage. I told them to write their names on the card phonetically so he could pronounce them correctly. I first grabbed Abdullah's card and told him to give me a pen, and I wrote, "AB DOO LAH - BIN SOO LA MEEN" on the card. Both Abdullahs protested because I'd misspelled their names as we walked up the stairs to Dumbledore. I told them, "Just hand him the card, dude." Dumbledore said their names perfectly.

Suddenly, I found myself about 10 feet from Dumbledore, and I realized I didn't fill out a card for myself, so I grabbed a card and simply wrote "Matt." After Dumbledore announced the woman in front of me with an intolerably long name, I handed him my card, and he merely announced "Matt?" as if it were a question. It took the crowd by surprise, and they erupted in laughter and applause. What kind of troglodyte only writes their first name? Does this guy think he's Prince? I raised my arms in victory and walked off the stage to a loud ovation.

"I'm fuckin' doing that!" Rex exploded, and my whole database class roared.

"No, you are fucking not!" I snapped back. "You promised!" Rex was undeterred and swore he would write only "Rex" on his card, get his applause, raise his arms, and have his day in the sun in front of a thousand graduating seniors. I pleaded with him and explained that I had paid for my graduate degree with my money, so I was free to do as I pleased, but your parents paid for your diploma, and they would be embarrassed and disappointed if they didn't hear their family's surname. I was relieved when Rex nodded in agreement and saw the logic in my argument. I said, "We're good, right?"

Rex nodded in agreement and softly said, "I'm fuckin' doin' it."

It was a colossal mistake to tell Rex of my graduation exploits, and I desperately wished I hadn't. I'd hoped there was no way he would write only "Rex." How could he? His mom and dad were there as well as his grandparents and siblings. Indeed, he would come to his senses. Of course, he wouldn't make me pay for my sin.

A few days later, I was deep in the shadowy bowels of an enormous arena that held thousands of people. All the professors in attendance changed into their Dumbledore and Snape gear, only to appear like third-world generals. The plan was to let the students settle in the vast arena, and then all of us Snapes and Dumbledores proceed down the middle aisle between the graduates, climb up on stage, and then drop into our places among the potted plants. I thought there was no way I could make a bad situation worse. Yes, I can; I am that idiot. I told two other professors whom I would be sitting with on stage among the Philodendron and ferns what I had done, looking for comfort and sympathy. Maybe it wouldn't be that bad if Rex went through with it, right? Maybe his mother wouldn't hunt me down after the ceremony and have me disbarred from ever teaching again.

The first professor I told doubled over in laughter, saying I was an idiot, and the other was not so charitable. In his mind, I should be banished to the snowy eastern tundra and mine salt the rest of my life for my mortal sins against academia.

Yevgeny barked in my ear as we walked up the aisle through the multitude of students, "How could you have been so thoughtless to recommend to one of our graduates to go through with such an insane plan and deeply embarrass our school and department," he said through his thick Russian accent. Even after settling in the potted plant forest, I told him to chill, but he wouldn't let it go. Fortunately for me, I put my earbuds in and settled into the sweet sounds of John Prine, which pissed Yevgeny off further, but he was satisfied to brood like a five-year-old and read a research paper he'd produced from under his robe.

After what seemed like the six millionth graduate crossed the stage and Prine was singing, "Blow up your TV, throw away your paper," I looked over to the stairs and saw a familiar face. Oh, shit! Rex was sporting a shit-eating grin, giving me the nod as I mouthed the words, "Don't. Do. It."

I heard him yell back, "Did you say do it." My Greek tragedy had commenced before my eyes, and there was nothing I could do to stop it. Rex handed Dumbledore his card, and he promptly announced in his bold voice, "Rex!" The graduates, moms, dads, and everyone in earshot went apeshit. Rex's moment had come, and it didn't disappoint. His arms went up as he acknowledged the cheering crowd. I looked over at the one professor as she was convulsing in laughter, and Yevgeny was turning red with anger.

We quickly walked back down the same aisle at the end of the ceremony with Yevgeny glued to my ear, telling me I didn't deserve to be wearing my sacred robe. As we turned the corner into the changing room in the bowels of the vast arena, Yevgeny and I almost ran into our dean, a smartly dressed, business savvy, former military man who kept the business school headed in the right direction. He looked directly at us and said, "Did you guys hear that Rex thing? That was fucking awesome!" Yevgeny shriveled as potted plants do, and I high-fived the dean. "Hell, yeah!"

Conclusion

That's all I can think of when it comes to succeeding at university after straw polling many colleagues, teachers, and countless students and recalling my college failures. What did I miss? Plenty, I'm sure. Either way, I hope this helped. Let me know if it did.

Best,
Matt

Important: What to Do if an Active Shooter Event Takes Place on Campus

I know this isn't college advice, but you need to hear it. God forbid an active shooter is on your campus. What do you do? The following is an article titled "**What to Do if an Active Shooter Event Takes Place on Campus?**" from the *Stevens Institute of Technology*.

Immediately upon hearing what may sound like gunshots or after being advised by others that an active shooter event is taking place and only if it is safe to do so, exit the building and seek shelter away from the area. Leaving the room or building should only be done if you can safely navigate your way out without confronting the shooter. Once you are safe, take the following steps:

1. Notify anyone you may encounter to avoid entering the building.
2. Encourage anyone who may safely exit the building to do so.
3. Evacuate to a safe area away from the danger and take protective cover. Stay there until assistance arrives.
4. Call your campus police department or dial 911, and provide the dispatcher with the following information:
   o Your name
   o The location where you believe the incident is taking place (be as specific as possible)
   o Number of shooters (if known)
   o Identification or description of shooter(s)
   o Your exact location
   o The number of people injured (if known)
5. Individuals not immediately affected by the situation should take protective cover, staying away from windows and doors until notified otherwise.

If you cannot safely exit the building, shelter in place by taking the following actions:

1. Go to the nearest room or office.
2. Close and lock the door, if possible.
3. Turn off the lights.
4. Seek protective cover.
5. Put your cellphone on silent (turn off vibrate mode). Keep quiet to give the appearance that no one is in the room.
6. Please do not answer the door unless you are sure it is the police.
7. Notify your campus police department or dial 911 if it is safe to do so, providing the dispatcher with the following information:
   o Your name
   o Your location (be as specific as possible)
   o The number of shooters
   o Identification or description of the shooter
   o Number of injured parties and their location (if known)
8. Wait for the police to assist you out of the building.

Made in the USA
Monee, IL
20 October 2022

ce7292c9-fc1c-4268-9433-297cdeeff7f4R01